A GUIDE TO AUSTRALIAN ROCKS, FOSSILS AND LANDSCAPES

More than 200 amazing geo-sites and landforms, from meteor craters to fossil beds

RUSSELL FERRETT

PREFACE

This book, *A Guide to Australian Rocks, Fossils and Landscapes*, contains information on hundreds of amazing geo-sites. But what is a geo-site? The answer is in the name: 'geo' means 'Earth' and of course 'site' is a specific place – it's an 'Earth site'. Lately, the 'geo' part has come to refer to geology, geography and/or geomorphology. There are thousands of geo-sites around Australia, but some are more interesting than others. I have chosen more than 200 of the most varied and intriguing examples to whet your appetite and hopefully generate interest.

These pages should not be viewed as scientific text designed to prep you for some grand examination. It's written in everyday English to assist inquisitive travellers and interested readers to understand the shaping of rocks and landforms in this wonderful country. You will not find extensive footnotes and references. The material for the book comes from personal observations, national park pamphlets, various specialised books, Google research, extensive travel, a university degree in geography and 40 years of teaching. There may be odd errors of fact contained within the writings; for these I apologise. I don't know where they are. If I did, I'd have corrected them.

Explanations of some geologic phenomena and processes are too large and/or complex, or common to too many sites to have them repeated in numerous sites. For these reasons, short segments have been written and inserted prior to relevant sites. In similar fashion, site numbers in parentheses (#) have been provided where relevant explanations can be found in commentaries related to other geo-sites.

Enjoy the book, and enjoy nature.

Russ Ferrett

CONTENTS

4

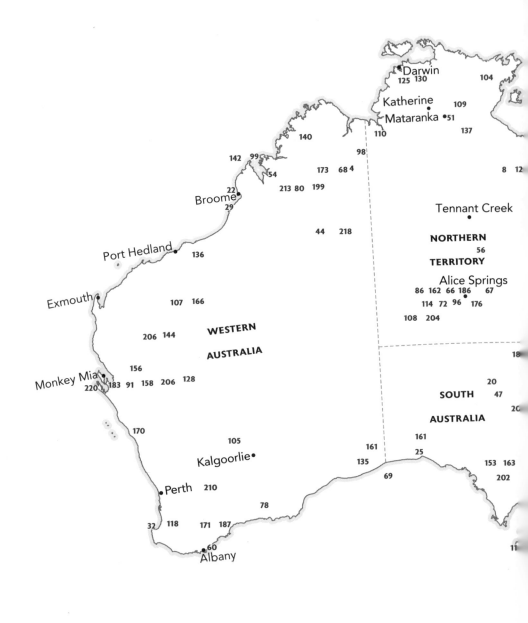

Darwin
125 130
104

Katherine
109
Mataranka •51
137

140
110

98

142 99
54
173 68 4
8 12

213 80 199

22
Broome
29

Tennant Creek •

44 218

NORTHERN
56
TERRITORY

Alice Springs
86 162 66 186 67
114 72 96 176
108 204

Port Hedland •
136

Exmouth •

107 166

WESTERN

206 144

AUSTRALIA

18

156

Monkey Mia •
220 183 91 158 206 128

20

SOUTH
47

AUSTRALIA
20

170

105

161

Kalgoorlie •
161
25

135

153 163
202

69

• Perth
210

78

32 118 171 187

11

• 60
Albany

N

0   300 km

Note: The scale on this map dictates that
positions shown are approximations only.

MAP OF SITES

87

Cooktown
15
43 9
Cairns
102 100 5
196 205 208 201
46

179 124
45
Mount Isa

74 Townsville

36 87

Longreach
58 81
70 87
Rockhampton
117

QUEENSLAND 38–39

77

175
37
52
83
Brisbane
85

02

41
71
18 6 212 133
Darling R. Bourke Armidale
Broken Hill 219 62 Coffs Harbour
138 167 19 182 76
NEW 134 65 160
SOUTH 211 193 57 Port Macquarie
17 34 27
122 3 79 121 188 191
131 106 103 189 21
WALES 197
2 214 26 101
delaide 120 73 11 83 9 Sydney
30 195 126 154 203 Wollongong
48 155 221 42 209
450 16 49 145 148 169 139 Canberra **A.C.T.** 53
143 151 **VICTORIA** 24 174 141 157
172 92 123 184 159 Eden 164
93 28 146 177 111 215
35 198 166 Melbourne
127 200
217

TASMANIA Launceston
Hobart

10 11 12 13 14 23 40
50 59 61 63 75 94 95
97 149 152 168 180
181 190 192 194 216

1. LIMESTONE

Limestone is a member of the calcite ($CaCO_3$) family. To be a member of that family, a rock must contain at least 50 per cent calcite. Other members include chalk, dolomite, gypsum, marble and tufa. Speleothems (cave formations) are almost pure calcite. Being a member of the family brings with it an inherited weakness; being dissolvable by weak acids.

Most limestones are formed as sedimentary layers on the floors of warm shallow seas or lakes where shells, dead corals and fish skeletons accumulate. Most people only see limestone once it has been raised above sea level, but there are huge amounts hidden below the waves.

Exposing limestone to rain starts a chemical reaction. Rain is slightly acidic.

As rain falls through the air it absorbs small amounts of carbon dioxide (CO_2), forming a very mild acid – carbonic acid. This acid dissolves the calcite in limestone; not much at any one time, but if you have sufficient rain or concentrated water flow, that 'not much' over a long period can grow to be enormous. This chemical weathering may result in the formation of features such as rills (top image), tunnels, arches or caves.

Most visitors heading to limestone country are not looking for surface features – they're after caves. Not the caves as such, but the rocks (speleothems) that grow in them. Speleothems are translucent crystals of calcite. This can be illustrated by shining a torch through one.

Speleothem growth is a process of deposition by precipitation. Precipitation in science means 'to come out of'. For example, if you leave a mug of coffee out in the air, the water component will evaporate and the coffee and sugar will precipitate in the bottom of the mug.

Precipitation of dissolved calcite is somewhat like that, but slightly more complex and much slower. Acidic water dissolves calcite because it is acidic, not because it's wet. If you lower the acidity of water containing calcite, it lowers that liquid's capacity to hold dissolved calcite. If the water is induced to return some of its CO_2 to the atmosphere, the solution's capacity to hold dissolved calcite is similarly reduced and precipitation takes place.

Evaporation may play a role, but as humidity in caves is normally high, rates of evaporation are generally low. Precipitation most often takes place where drips of water containing dissolved calcite form on cave roofs, on floors where drips fall, along seepage cracks, under shallow flowing water and from other wet surfaces including already formed speleothems.

2. ABERCROMBIE CAVES

Abercrombie's greatest claim to fame is its Archway; supposedly the largest natural bridge in the Southern Hemisphere. The Archway's tunnel/cave can be walked as a self-guided tour. It is well lit and easy to negotiate. The Abercrombie Caves have not been funded or staffed to the same level as many other cave systems. Guided tours are restricted mainly to weekends and school holidays.

The Abercrombie Caves are in marble (image below). The marble was formed by pressure applied to the original limestone during the Lachlan Folding period (**#116**); a period when it was downfolded and compressed. The fact that the rock is marble makes little difference to the speleothems. Marble suffers from the same weakness as limestone; it dissolves in weak acids. When the dissolved marble is precipitated, the precipitate is calcite; exactly the same as from limestone.

A recent rock fall (2018), where Grove Creek spills out through the Archway, has closed the quick-and-easy method of viewing the Archway Cave system. You can no longer walk to the river exit point, walk through the cave/tunnel to its natural entrance, turn around and return the same way. You now must walk over the hill to the cave's natural entrance, walk through it, turn around and retrace your steps. But there are some advantages beyond that of improved fitness to be had from the forced extra walking. The outside walk takes you past fluted marble and dolines. The marble is white as it does not oxidise as readily as limestone. Dolines are funnel-shaped depressions that form on the surface where underlying caverns have collapsed. Inside the 200m-long Archway there are a wide variety of common speleothems such as stalagmites, columns, straws and shawls. Grove Creek flows through the cave with sufficient depth to permit the passage of fish. A mid-tunnel bridge allows walkers to cross from one side to the other.

The Arch Cave also has human history. It was used by the Wirradjuri and Gundungurra Groups for thousands of years. Much later, during early colonisation, bushrangers used the caves for hideouts, and in the late 1800s gold miners constructed a dance floor below the Archway for social events. The original was destroyed, but later rebuilt. It is still there.

Above: River entry to Abercrombie's Archway Cave.   Below: River exit.

3. AGE OF FISHES

We could say the fish were dead unlucky. If the rains had fallen a few days earlier they may have survived. But that was 360 million years ago.

The rains did come and fine silt washed into the lake covering the dead fish laying in the mud at the bottom. Birds had not yet evolved to scavenge the carcasses and there were no land animals either; they were still millions of years away. This was the Age of Fishes.

But luck changes. A road worker operating a bulldozer in 1956 unearthed a stone. On turning it over he noted its odd appearance and pushed it to one side. The rock had split along the line where the fresh sand had covered the dead fish. Later the rock was identified as containing the fossilised shapes of dead fish. It was displayed in the Australian Museum in Sydney from 1966 to 2006. A proper archaeological dig was not undertaken at the site until 1993. It was only then that scientists realised the enormity of the find. This was one of the greatest fossil finds of the 20th century.

The initial slab, now referred to as 'the 1956 slab', was returned to Canowindra in 2006. This single slab alone contained fossil moulds of at least 100 fish. The Canowindra fossils are very different to those of large bony creatures such as dinosaurs, where silica and other minerals have seeped into the skeletons replacing the original bony material.

The Canowindra fossils are negative moulds. That is, all the original flesh and bones have gone; all that remains are the vacant spaces that were once occupied by the dead fish. Plaster poured into these moulds provides near-perfect replicas of the original inhabitants that occupied the spaces. Towards the centre of the 1956 slab is a fossil of *Canowindra grossi* (image above). The fish had a dual breathing system, having both lungs and gills. It also had fleshy, rounded fins and was around 55cm long. In later digs no further fossils of this fish have been unearthed.

There's a lot more to the Age of Fishes Museum than *Canowindra grossi*. Other fossils collected from the dig site are also featured in the exhibition along with full-sized models and detailed information.

The internally housed collection is supplemented by an outstanding outdoor display of fossil slabs from the 1993 excavations. The dig site is less than half an hour's drive from Canowindra Museum. Maps are available. The site is at the side of a local gravel road. Scavenging is not permitted.

4. ARGYLE DIAMOND MINE

The Argyle diamonds were transported to the surface by a volcanic plume that originated in the Earth's lower mantle. The plume was of lamproite – a type of rock that has little economic value except that it occasionally contains diamonds.

Diamonds form in isolated regions of the upper mantle. In Argyle's case, the lamproite plume simply passed through such a region and acted as an elevator transporting the diamonds to the surface. The diamonds are thought to have formed around 400 million years prior to being transported to the surface.

On nearing the surface the lamproite plume encountered water that instantly turned to steam, blasting out a volcanic pipe. Fallen broken rocky material and blobs of lamproite lava (collectively called tuff) fell back into and around the hole forming a ring, termed a maar.

Since its creation the Argyle Maar has been significantly reduced in size by erosion. At the surface, the lamproite tuff has a thin tadpole shape nearly 2km long; 100–300m wide in its tail section and 500m across at its head. Below the tuff, and below the level of open-pit mining, is the solid lamproite pipe. The number, size and quality of diamonds contained within the tuff is greater than

those found in the lamproitic pipe. This is due to the rapid ascent and cooling of the diamonds contained in the initial eruptions. Those that were carried in later eruptions travelled more slowly towards the surface and were

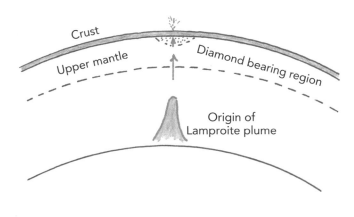

subject to resorption. Resorption is the process that diamonds can be subject to during the lava solidification process whereby they are reformed as graphite.

The Argyle Diamond Mine is by volume the largest producer of diamonds in the world. Total production since 1983 is approaching 200 tonnes. It is anticipated that mining after 2021 will become uneconomic. Argyle's average diamond size is small, but it produces more than 90 per cent of the world's ultra-expensive pink and red diamonds.

5. ATHERTON WATERFALL CIRCUIT

Millaa Millaa, Zillie and Ellinjaa Falls (left to right, below) can be reached via the Waterfall Circuit that leaves the Palmerston Highway 2km east of Millaa Millaa. These three falls are perhaps the prettiest and certainly the most accessible on the Atherton Tableland.

The tableland with its steep slopes and high rainfall is perfect for the formation of waterfalls. The highest falls are found on the eastern side of the plateau where rivers plunge from the tableland to the coastal plain. However, many waterfalls are slightly inland where rivers flow over the edges of lava flows. The three pictured above belong to this group.

The Atherton Tableland lies over a volcanic plume that became active approximately 4 million years ago. The plume is probably still present beneath the surface, but currently doing nothing and may be dying. This plume spawned more than 50 volcanic outlets that blanketed the plateau with hundreds of separate lava flows of varying thicknesses.

The Millaa Millaa Waterfall tumbles over at least three such lava flows. The vertical columns of solidified basalt are most obvious in the lowest of the lava flows exposed at the back of the plunge pool.

6. ARKAROOLA RIDGE TOP

The Ridgetop Tour costs, but no one complains after having done it. The ridge-top road was built by mineral exploration companies after having their creek-crossing roads regularly washed out following rains. The spectacular road is not open to private vehicles, and after

you've experienced the tour you'll understand why. It's not for the faint hearted either, or for those hoping for a plush ride in a limousine. It's great. Each tour to Sillers Lookout (left) and back takes four and a half hours. The tea, coffee and lamington at the lookout are good, but the trees as toilets are primitive.

At the northern end of the Flinders Ranges, Arkaroola is a privately owned sanctuary established by one of Australia's greatest geologists and discoverer of the Ediacaran fossils (**#64**), Reg Sprigg. The nature sanctuary, resort, campground and information office continues to be run by his family. Very little mining ever occurred at Arkaroola and it is now totally prohibited by law.

Arkaroola is a geologist's Disneyland. It has all the rocks, colours and steep slopes of other parts of the Flinders, but with the added variation of an intruded mass of granite with its associated injection of a huge variety of minerals. Great columns of colourful rocks rear out of the hills. This is one of the world's greatest natural collections of rocks and minerals. Geologists from all over come here for study and research, or just to ogle.

The land is rough. It's what geographers call 'all slopes terrain'. There's no flat land on the tops of hills and no flat land at the bottoms. It's difficult to find a place to stand where one foot is not higher or lower than the other. So just walk or sit, photograph and enjoy.

7. AUSTRALIA'S EARLY GEOLOGY

Australia may be very old in general, but that is not the case for all of it. Nearly all the land south-east of a bendy line from Adelaide to Townsville is younger than 600 million years of age. It is to South Australia and Western Australia you should head if looking for really old rocks.

Considered to be one of Earth's oldest rocks is a 4.4-billion-year-old fragment of an otherwise worthless zircon, discovered some 150km north-west of Meekatharra in Western Australia (**#156**). As the Earth is only 4.6 billion years old, you're not going to find anything much older. But something smaller than a grain of sand hardly makes a continent!

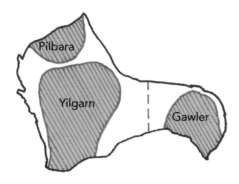

Australia's true beginning dates from around 2.7 billion years ago with the accidental bumping together of drifting pieces of older, pre-existing, granitic sections of crust, termed terranes. They formed what are now known as the Yilgarn and Pilbara Cratons in Western Australia and the Gawler Craton of South Australia. Cratons are large blocks of stable crust. These accidental collisions produced Australia Mark I (left).

A much-improved Mark II version (right) was produced around a billion years later; but it lacked a few basics. Huge masses of granite were injected below parts of present-day northern Queensland and across into the Northern Territory. These granites, together with surrounding ancient metamorphic rocks, formed a fourth craton.

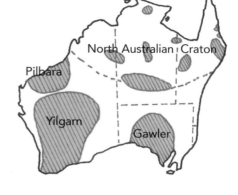

These four cratons are the underpinning of the Australian Continent. Like rich modern-day tourists these cratons, stitched together by other rock, travelled the Earth, crossing the Equator several times and even making it to the North Pole. Driven by mantle currents beneath the crust, the cratons travelled

Rocks folded deep below the surface before being exposed at Harveys Return, Kangaroo Island.

free of charge; but if they had had to pay, they certainly could afford it. These cratons contain most of Australia's gold, silver, lead, uranium, iron, diamonds and other valuable minerals, but not coal or natural gas. Granite (**#55**) is at the core of all continents. It is the core because it is the least dense (lightest) of the igneous rocks and tends to 'float' on other igneous rocks such as basalt (**#33**). Igneous rocks are those that solidify from a molten state. Basalt forms a rocky floor to the great oceans while granite, along with sedimentaries, comprise the bulk of continents. For those who wish to know: the specific gravity (weight) of water is 1g/cm^3; the specific gravity of granite is $2.6–2.7\text{g/cm}^3$, and that of basalt is $2.8–3.0\text{g/cm}^3$.

Around a billion years ago, Australia bumped into and became attached to Antarctica, making for Australia Mk III (Gondwana Mk I).

8. BARKLY TABLELAND

You can choose a thousand near-identical geo-sites on the Barkly. I've chosen one 130km north of Barkly Homestead on the Tablelands Highway where that road crosses Brunette Creek.

This area is part of the ancient Georgina Basin. Mountain-building squeezes and/or volcanic activity have been absent here for hundreds of millions of years. It has been lifted up as if by a giant helicopter. Elevation at this site is 220m. As far as the eye can see the difference between highest and lowest points is generally less than 20m and slopes, where you can find them, are less than 1°.

Most geologic interest here is in the soil. It's black clay that can be metres thick. The black colouring is humus from decayed grass having not completely rotted away. This is due to insufficient rainfall. As the heavy clay soil dries out over 'winter', it shrinks forming cracks wide enough for you to thrust your fist and forearm down full length without reaching the bottom. With the onset of

the wet-season rains, water fills the cracks, the clay expands and the soil becomes sealed again.

Excess water floods the land, but eventually finds its way into Brunette Creek (above). The creek drains south-west into several ephemeral lakes. The dominant vegetation is a mix of Mitchell and Flinders Grasses.

9. BARRON RIVER WATERFALL

Here exposed on a grand scale is the classic heavyweight conflict – running water versus granite. Rivers running over granite seldom (never?) develop vertical waterfalls. The 260m-high Barron Falls are a braided mix of steeply inclined segments, sluggish pools and tumbling rapids. Such waterfalls are commonly referred to as

horsetails. Their size and lack of symmetry makes them difficult to photograph in their entirety, unless from a helicopter or a Sky Rail gondola.

The fragmentation of the falls is a result of granite's style of disintegration and erosion (**#55**). The river utilises the weakness of granite's joints by, in places, removing whole blocks of stone that were once squeezed between others. In addition, it continually dislodges individual crystals of quartz and feldspar from the solid granite by slow attrition. This process is very slow and results in the smoothing of surfaces.

The in-between pools mark places where groups of adjacent blocks have been removed. Piles of these blocks can be seen around the edge of the pool and at the foot of the falls.

The granite intrusion occurred almost 300 million years ago. Much later, around 100 million to 55 million years ago, an upwelling below the crust caused the region to dome, raising the granite and land to the west. At the same time, areas east of

the granite stretched. These areas gradually subsided below sea level, forming what is referred to as the Queensland Plateau – a near-flat area that towers above the floor of the adjacent Coral Sea.

Aggressive river erosion has removed much of the land between the coast and the granite, and by doing so has formed the Great Escarpment (**#101**). That escarpment, due to its straightness, is often incorrectly identified as a fault line. There are a number of actual faults in this region with some running close to north-south, but none are responsible for the Great Escarpment. The escarpment is due to erosion alone. The Barron Gorge is a continuation of these same erosional processes.

10. BATMAN BRIDGE

It's not the bridge we're looking at; it's the geology behind the engineering decision to use this pleasant-to-the-eye bridge shape to span the Tamar Estuary. The bridge's shape is a brilliant and architecturally neat solution to a geological problem. It was Australia's first cable-stayed bridge.

The problem faced by engineers was that the eastern bank of the estuary (left side in the photograph below) was underlain by degraded and loose rock.

Around 30 million years ago a volcanic eruption to the north of the bridge, near East Arm, flowed basalt lava to the south-west and under what is now the eastern end of Batman Bridge. However, the lava flow was shallow and less than 5m thick at this point. Further geological inspection indicated that the thin basalt flow rested on deeply compacted mud, sand and volcanic ash; a base unsuited for the foundations of a major bridge. Further inspection however, concluded that the western bank of dolerite (**#12**) was solid and would provide a suitable base for the bridge.

The A-frame is near the western end of the bridge and, with the use of cables, supports 78 per cent of the bridge's total weight. The bridge is built of steel, as steel is easier to use and lighter than concrete.

The bridge's basic dimensions are:

Overall length: 432m   Clearance for shipping: 28m
River span: 215m   Height of A-frame: 95m above mean river height.
Inclination of A-frame: 20° off vertical.

11. BAY OF FIRES

The bay, north of St Helens and stretching between Binalong Bay and Eddystone Point, was named by Tobias Furneaux in 1773 after seeing the fires of Aborigines on the beach. Furneaux was the captain of HMS *Adventure* and part of Captain Cook's second voyage of exploration.

The granite here is part of the fractured but related bodies – including Wilsons

Promontory, Flinders Island, Mount William, Bay of Fires, St Helens, Freycinet Peninsula and Maria Island – that formed well below the surface 400 million to 360 million years ago. These granites are of various colours, but in the Bay of Fires they're basically grey.

The main constituents of granite are quartz (silica oxide, SiO_2), feldspar and mica. The grey colouring is in the feldspar. Feldspar breaks down to very fine particles of clay and it, together with the mica, has been washed out. The white sand is simply the weathered and eroded quartz component of the granite.

The spectacular orange colour on the rocks around the Bay of Fires is lichen (pronounced 'like-n'). Lichen are composite things; a symbiotic relationship between either algae or cyanobacteria with a fungus. They are not plants. Any plain grey colouring on the rocks, and occasionally near the lichen, is algae.

12. TASMANIA'S DOLERITE

Around 170 million years ago and coinciding with the initial break-up of Gondwana, large scale melting of the upper mantle and lower crust occurred beneath Tasmania. Great volumes of magma rose from the mantle and pushed up into the sandstones that covered much of the eastern half of the present-day island.

The magma, however, did not reach the surface but forced its way along weak bedding planes that lay between different strata of sandstone.

As pressure from the dense (heavy) magma flow increased, the bedding planes separated and the sandstone above the dolerite rose upward to 'float' on the intrusion.

The eventual thickness of the magma reached 300–350m. When the flow of magma ceased, it cooled to form massive dolerite sills (horizontal injections of covered lava). Cooling took millennia as the molten mass was insulated from the cooling effect of the atmosphere by the sandstone that covered it. As the magma cooled it contracted and formed vertical cracks and columns as is common in basalt (**#33**). These columns reached the full depth of the dolerite sills, that is, with lengths of up to 350m.

For more than a 100 million years the dolerites and the sandstones were buffeted by earthquakes, vertical rises and falls in the Earth's crust, plus some sideways jostling, folding and faulting. The Earth experienced a number of ice ages and there was significant erosion by running water. All of these changed Tasmania's surface. Virtually all the overlying sandstone was removed together with much of the dolerite and even some of the underlying sandstone.

The remaining dolerite now forms cappings to much of south-eastern, central and north-eastern parts of the island. The map (top right) indicates the area initially intruded by the dolerite. Although a relatively small state, Tasmania has the world's largest exposure of dolerite.

Dolerite cliffs at Cape Hauy.

13. BEN LOMOND CLIFFS

Ben Lomond is a 1,300–1,400m-high dolerite plateau
surrounded by faults and cliffs. Ben Lomond's cliffs display one
of Tasmania's most historical geological events; the injection of
dolerite. Dolerite has the same chemical composition as basalt, but has a slightly
larger crystal size due to its slower rate of cooling.

During the ice ages, Ben Lomond must have been spectacular. Perhaps not so
much during the last ice stage which was less severe, but the one before, about
40,000–50,000 years ago.
Ice then would have flowed
over the gap that is now
Jacobs Ladder and down the
mountainside. Information
boards have been erected
at the remnants of an early
moraine (below right) that can
be viewed at the rest stop a
short distance before the road
ascends Jacobs Ladder.

In winter, Ben Lomond
experiences periglacial
conditions with snow and sub-
zero temperatures. Not cold
enough to form glaciers, but
sufficiently cold to freeze water

The pale patch on the cliff at Jacobs Ladder was caused
by a cluster of columns recently breaking away and falling
from the main body of dolerite.

held in the numerous cracks of dolerite. As water freezes to form ice it expands
by about 10 per cent. In doing so it loosens the rock columns, causes some to split
and form grotesque shapes, and others to lean dangerously (below left) or even fall.

14. BICHENO BLOWHOLE

The east-coast Tasmanian town of Bicheno boasts a number of culinary, historical and accommodation highlights, as well has some great natural attractions. A cluster of these are grouped around its blowhole.

The blowhole is effective in drenching unsuspecting viewers and makes for fine photographs, particularly when paired with its adjacent rock. This is granite country (**#55**) with its gridded joint lines washed clean and the surface made smooth and slippery. The blowhole entrance is at the apex of a small V shaped niche that directs waves from the Tasman Sea directly into the blowhole's entrance. The size of each blow is controlled by the size of waves rather than compression of air as at Kiama in New South Wales (**#113**).

The huge adjacent granite block, perhaps 50 tonnes or more, is an enigma. How did it get there? It's unlikely that the block rests there because the blocks surrounding it have eroded away. It appears to have been placed there by a huge ocean wave. Some geologists suggest that the rock is evidence that the east coast of Australia has in the past been struck by tsunami (tidal waves).

On a much smaller scale to the above are the numerous small pools of salt found on the landward side of the blowhole. When winds blow from east, which is common, blowhole spray falls inland. Under warm sunny conditions and light breezes, the fine spray is partly evaporated before falling to ground forming shallow pools. Water in the pools also evaporates rapidly under these conditions. This results in pools of salt up to 1cm thick (above left).

15. BLACK MOUNTAIN

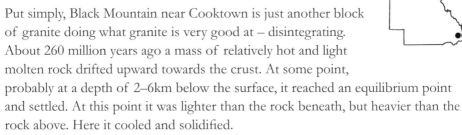

Put simply, Black Mountain near Cooktown is just another block of granite doing what granite is very good at – disintegrating. About 260 million years ago a mass of relatively hot and light molten rock drifted upward towards the crust. At some point, probably at a depth of 2–6km below the surface, it reached an equilibrium point and settled. At this point it was lighter than the rock beneath, but heavier than the rock above. Here it cooled and solidified.

Over the next couple of hundred million years this part of Queensland was pushed and/or floated up by more than 8,000m. Some of the later uplift was associated with the formation of the Great Dividing Range. The lifting of the landmass above sea level led to rapid erosion of the rock above the granite intrusion. This in turn lightened  the landmass which caused it to float even higher. These processes of forced uplift, flotation and erosion eventually saw the rock above the intrusion totally removed and the granite exposed.

The exposed granite expanded, fractured and weathered to form the mountain we see today. Beneath this covering of boulders lie much larger boulders and below that again is almost solid granite. Best have a look at (**#55**) for more detail.

With granite's components breaking down to become sand, clay, and shiny mica flakes, you might expect Black Mountain to be covered by soil. Perhaps if it was less steep that may be true. But here near Cooktown, the slope is steep and rainfall heavy. Surface run-off washes away any soil that manages to form.

Oops! I almost forgot. The black colouring is caused by a thin covering of blue-green algae growing on the rocks.

16. BLUE LAKE COMPLEX

The region around Mount Gambier is the most likely area in
Australia to experience the next volcanic eruption. Not that
this revelation should cause a sharp drop in property values
or increased anxiety among the city's inhabitants. The last eruption, arguably
Australia's most recent, has a dated minimum at around 4,300 years. If and
when the next volcanic eruption occurs, it will be heralded by numerous shallow
earthquakes. So leave the worrying until then and go take a look.

Mount Gambier's volcano is Australia's only urban volcano. At lunchtime
workers in the city can sit at its edge, eat their sangers and gaze out over Blue Lake
pondering when it will next change colour. Being urban, the volcanic complex has
the usual accoutrements: public toilets, paved parking, picnic areas, park benches
and potable water; a volcano with a five-star rating.

Blue Lake is approximately 1km wide, has a flattish bottom and an average
depth of 70m. During the cooler months of April to November the water is a
sombre grey colour, but in summer from November to March it is a vibrant blue.
The colour change is thought to be chemical in nature. As the weather warms
in summer, microscopic crystals of calcium carbonate form on the surface. The
crystals scatter the blue wavelengths of daylight giving the lake its cobalt colour.
In winter when surface temperatures fall and the lake water is stirred by greater
inflows, the crystals disappear leaving the water murky and grey. All the lakes,
the city's main tourist attraction and water supply, sit in volcanic craters. They are
maars (**#177** and **198**).

Around 4,300–5,000 years ago, heat from rising lava came in contact with the
water-bearing limestone that underlies Mount Gambier. The ground water, held
under pressure by the rock above, was heated to temperatures well above 100°C.
At critical points in time the rock gave way and the water instantly turned to steam
blasting the overlying rock skywards forming the huge holes.

Opposite above: Image looking south-south-east across the site. Leg of Mutton is hidden while
Brownes Lake comprises the two small dark patches at the bottom right of the photo.

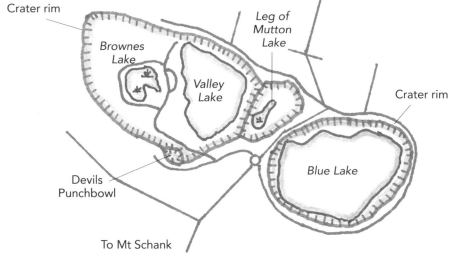

Crater rim

Brownes
Lake

Leg of
Mutton
Lake

Valley
Lake

Crater rim

Blue Lake

Devils
Punchbowl

To Mt Schank

17. BORDER CLIFFS

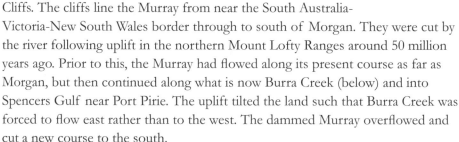

Headings Cliffs Lookout (opposite), near Renmark-Paringa, is one of the best locations to view a section of the Murray's Border Cliffs. The cliffs line the Murray from near the South Australia-Victoria-New South Wales border through to south of Morgan. They were cut by the river following uplift in the northern Mount Lofty Ranges around 50 million years ago. Prior to this, the Murray had flowed along its present course as far as Morgan, but then continued along what is now Burra Creek (below) and into Spencers Gulf near Port Pirie. The uplift tilted the land such that Burra Creek was forced to flow east rather than to the west. The dammed Murray overflowed and cut a new course to the south.

And that wasn't the end of it. From 25 million to 11 million years ago the lower Murray was flooded by the ocean, and limestone beds were laid down covering the pre-existing surface. The Murray, during this interlude, flowed into this shallow ocean well upstream from Mildura. Renewed uplift along the Mount Lofty Ranges saw the lower Murray region exposed with the River Murray returning to an earlier course by flowing west to Morgan and then turning south.

The cliff sections are on the outside banks of huge meanders. The Murray River, having cut down to a point where its bed is now almost horizontal, is now widening its valley by snaking backwards and forwards across it to create an alluvial plain. Rivers run fastest on the outside of bends, eroding the soft young limestone. The flat and low-lying land on the inside of each meander is the end result of the river's manoeuvres.

18. BRACHINA GORGE

About 500 million years ago the Flinders Ranges' rivers would have run along the bottoms of synclines (downfolds), but as time passed and erosion proceeded, the drainage pattern changed to one where some rivers cut across the north-south ridge lines to flow east or

west onto the plains. Brachina Creek is one such stream and by cutting across the folded sediment it exposes 120 million years of rock history. The gravel road through Brachina Gorge runs alongside the creek and in places along the creek bed itself. High-clearance two-wheel-drive vehicles can make the 20km (one way) trip as long as there hasn't been recent rain.

The road crosses 12 major rock formations. Junctions between each are marked by information panels. It is suggested you buy a *Brachina Gorge Geological Trail* brochure at Wilpena Pound or other information places before you take the drive. This will give you geological information as well as a map that indicates where information boards are located. It is recommended that the trip be taken starting in the morning and travelling from east to west.

Elatina, the second stop on the drive, is an example of the geological formations encountered. Elatina contains evidence of a 620-million-years-ago ice age. Glaciers creeping out of the Gawler Ranges flowed into the shallow sea that was the Adelaide Geosyncline. There they melted and

dropped their load of erratics, stones, sand and gravel. (Erratics are rocks brought from one location and deposited in a different location.) These glacial deposits (right) eventually hardened into rock termed tillite that also outcrops in many other places in the ranges. The site for viewing the tillite is well marked.

19. BREADKNIFE

The Breadknife is a stunning example of a volcanic dyke. It lies within the Warrumbungle National Park. The dyke is over 500m long, almost 90m high and only 4–5m thick. The smaller photo (below left) was taken from the uphill end of the dyke.

We know that it is a dyke because the trachyte (**#33**) columns that comprise the landform are lying horizontal. When lava cools in a lava flow, it shrinks forming vertical columns from the coldest surface down to the bottom. When lava is forced into a crack within ash or older lava, the coldest surfaces are at the sides of the cracks. Hence the fine cracks run from the cold edges towards the centre of the intruded dyke. These columns, lying on their sides, can be clearly seen near both the top and the bottom of the main photo (right).

The Breadknife is reached by the Grand High Tops walk that begins at the park's information centre. The walk is 14km and quite strenuous; but takes you past and provides views to some of the finest volcanic scenery in the world. Climbing the Breadknife is strictly prohibited.

20. BREAKAWAYS

To the west of the Simpson Desert (**#185**), north from Coober Pedy (**#47**) and into the Northern Territory is an arid gibber plain dotted by low hills or 'jump-ups' as they are referred to by locals. They provided great backdrops for the shooting of films such as some of the *Mad Max* series.

The rock formation responsible for these flat-topped hills is part of the Great Artesian Basin series. These rocks are near-horizontally bedded, lie on the western edge of the basin and are 150–200m higher than Lake Eyre. With an uplift 60 million years ago, these sedimentary layers became exposed to weathering and erosion. Various minerals, particularly iron oxide, were carried down through the then soil to enter and collect in the top layer of sandstone. The iron oxide filled the gaps between the grains in the sandstone making it impervious and much harder and more resistant to the normal processes of weathering and erosion. This thin layer of sandstone became what is now referred to as duricrust. When the covering soil was removed by erosion, the duricrust remained as resistant strata. Over time, and in climatic conditions quite different to those of today, streams cut through the duricrust to another resistant layer below. The valleys quickly broadened by undercutting the duricrust. The remnants of the original duricrust now stand above the surrounding plain as low hills.

A 60km circuit out of and north of Coober Pedy leads you past the Breakaways. They are best photographed either early in the morning or in the two to three hours before sunset.

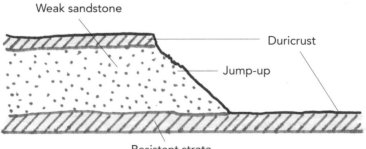

21. BROKEN BAY

Unlike Sydney Harbour, Broken Bay has no flat land at the western end of its inlet. The Hawkesbury (Nepean) is an antecedent river. That is, it existed before the present landscape evolved. Before the uplift of the Blue Mountains the Nepean-Hawkesbury followed a leisurely path to the ocean at Broken Bay. The uplift north of Penrith potentially blocked the river's run to the sea. But the volume of water in the Hawkesbury together with the softness of the underlying sandstone permitted the river to cut down through the rock at the same speed as the mountain building was raising its bed. This allowed the river to continue flowing along its old course.

In the last ice ages, sea level fell by as much as 130m. During those times the Hawkesbury River cut a deep gorge through what is now Broken Bay to reach the ocean. When sea levels again rose to their current height, Broken Bay was inundated with the ocean extending inland to Yarramundi, 140km upstream from the Hawkesbury's former mouth. Only during flood time does the Hawkesbury River's flow overcome the daily ups and downs of ocean tides. Broken Bay is no longer being deepened; it's filling with sand and gravel.

Its location close to Sydney and the presence of deep water right up to the shore make Broken Bay an ideal playground for boaties.

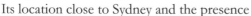
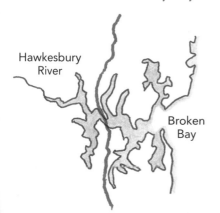

Hawkesbury River

Broken Bay

You could say that the Nepean-Hawkesbury is maladjusted. The Nepean rises in gently rolling hill-land far to the south, flows through deep gorges to emerge onto a fertile flood plain only to have a name change, and run through another gorge system before directly entering the sea without the usual surrounding coastal flats.

22. BROOME'S DINOSAUR COAST

North from Broome and stretching to Cape Leveque is the recently named, 'Dinosaur Coast'. It's an area of sweeping

Cape Leveque.

beaches, rocky headlands, broken cliffs and few tourists. Those that do come are mainly looking for evidence of dinosaurs that lived here 130 million years ago.

Researchers have identified more than 20 different types of tracks (footprints) ranging in size from 20–170 cm; the largest from a huge sauropod, a meat eater. This is the most diverse range of tracks to be found anywhere in the world. The largest track (below right) is approximately 250mm from the tip of the inside toe to the tip of the outside one. The photo was taken just north of Broome.

The trackways are not only of interest to geologists, they are culturally significant to the Aboriginal People of the north-west where they are part of the Dreamtime. Most of the tracks are remote and those being studied are 'out-of-bounds' to tourists. But if you wish to view some tracks talk to the people at the Information Office and also ask around tourist guides that frequent the Information Office area.

All photos: Carol Moore.

23. BRUNY ISLAND TOMBOLO

Bruny Island has probably the best tombolo that you will ever see.
A tombolo? It's a sand strip built by constructive waves (**#84**) that
bridges a gap between two islands or between an island and the mainland. In this
case it's island to island – South Bruny to North Bruny.

The tombolo began building at the end of the ice ages. With sea levels as much
as 130m below current levels, the two islands became insignificant rocky ridges
and part of the Tasmanian mainland, which in turn was part of the Australian
mainland. As the climate warmed, sea levels rose both separating Tasmania from
the mainland and two highest tops of the Bruny Ridges from themselves and also
the island of Tasmania. The greatest distance between the two islands prior to the
formation of the tombolo was more than 7km.

Waves coming from the south, on reaching the southern end of South Bruny
would split with part to the west of the island and the other part to the east. On

reaching the northern end of Bruny South the waves
would sweep around, meet, lose momentum and drop
their loads of sand to the floor of the passage separating
the islands. The deposition of sand built spits both at the
northern end of South Bruny and the southern end of
North Bruny. The two spits gradually merged to form the
tombolo.

The narrow section of the tombolo is around 1.5km
long. The road along the tombolo section is gravel to
encourage penguins to cross.

24. BUCHAN CAVES

Buchan Caves have all the usual features of limestone caves, including stalactites, stalagmites, columns, flowstones and more, but somehow it's different; it's just more intimate. It's a little off the beaten track, but becomes very popular on weekends, particularly if the weather's foul at Lakes Entrance and tourists from there flee to the caves seeking a rain- and windproof diversion. You are up close and personal to everything; too close for the health of some of the prize exhibits. Many of the walkways are narrow and netting barriers have been provided to stop you accidently brushing against stalagmites, stalagmites or columns. There are many steps, but fortunately most are downwards as the cave exit is lower than its entrance. Even if you are not a great lover of caves how could you not but be affected by the sheer beauty of the cavern shown in the image (below). It has formed near to the entrance of Royal Cave.

Around 450 million years ago south-east Australia was nothing but groups of scattered volcanic islands in a deepish sea. Deposits of sediment gradually settled between the islands to become shale, mudstone, tuff (cemented volcanic ash) and, as the seas became shallower and warmer, limestone. The Buchan limestone is around 400 million years old. The oldest of the 300–350m-thick beds contain few fossils but have progressively more towards the top. The Buchan Caves limestone abuts and covers the sides of some of the underlying ancient volcanic islands that now form part of the Snowy River Ranges. The whole area was caught up in the uplifts caused by the intrusion of granites in the region and the folding and faulting of the Lachlan Folding event (#116) around 450–350 million years ago.

The caves first formed as an underground river. At that time there were no fancy decorations as the running and sometimes flooding water would have washed clean the floor, sides and roofs of the caves. Later, the river formed a new and lower course that robbed the upper course of its main water supply. It is this older, now reasonably dry section of the underground river that is open to visits by the general public.

25. BUNDA CLIFFS

The Nullarbor is the world's largest body of limestone. It dates back to the time of Australia's separation from Antarctica beginning around 100 million years ago. As Australia drifted north the crust between the separating continents stretched and thinned. The central southern part of the Australian continent sagged, dipping gently towards Antarctica. By 50 million years ago the area now covered by the Nullarbor Plain lay beneath a shallow sea. It remained under the sea for the next 15 million years and during that time built a thick layer of limestone from the skeletons of dead shellfish, bryozoans and algae. This rock, up to 300m thick, is Wilson Bluff Limestone and can be seen along the cliffs as the bright white layer immediately

above the waves. Much more of this stratum lies below sea level than above it. This first limestone-building period ended with the onset of an earlier ice age that saw sea levels fall dramatically and the emergence of the Nullarbor Plain.

From about 35 million years ago through to 10 million years ago the Earth went through several ice ages interspersed with warmer and drier conditions. Sea levels rose and fell and the Nullarbor oscillated between being dry land and ocean floor. During this period, two major deposits of limestone occurred. First the Abrakurrie Limestone Series, a dark brown layer up to 90m thick, and after that, a thinner and younger layer referred to as the Nullarbor Series. It is the weathered Nullarbor Series limestone that now forms much of the surface of the plain. Along the Bunda Cliffs, where the land surface plunges vertically more than 100m into the sea, much of the youngest limestone has been removed so that the cliffs show two colours only: the white of the oldest layer, and above it the brown of the middle layer.

26. BUNGONIA SLOT CANYON

Limestone at Bungonia Gorge, near Marulan in New South
Wales, is unlike that found on the broad Nullarbor Plain of
central Australia where it extends for hundreds of kilometres.
Here at Bungonia the limestone stratum has been folded so that instead of being
horizontal it now sits almost on end and pointing to the sky. The folding occurred
between 450 million and 340 million years ago as part of the Lachlan Fold event

(**#116**). At Bungonia the limestone is sandwiched between
sandstones, siltstones, shales and in some places, ancient
volcanic rock.

Bungonia Creek, a minor tributary of the Shoalhaven
River, starts life on the plateau, runs across inclined layers
of other sedimentaries before crossing the limestone and
tumbling down to join the Shoalhaven. In the photo (left),
the creek is running from bottom left to top right. Also,
note the flatness of the horizon in the photograph.) Not
only did the creek run across the top of the limestone, water
from it leaked down between cracks that had formed during
the folding. Continual dissolving of the rock formed caves
and caverns below the stream bed. Repetitive roof collapses
and further dissolving of the limestone has allowed the creek to lower its bed to its
present location, 350m below the level of the plateau. Now that Bungonia Creek
has reached this lower level the limestone walls are relatively dry and dissolving
of the limestone there by solution has almost ceased. Dry limestone is incredibly
strong and resistant to rock slides and other mass movement, hence the steepness
of the canyon. Downstream from the canyon, the valley walls have been carved
into weaker rocks. Slopes there are still steep, but not precipitous as in the canyon.

A very steep walking trail allows fit and careful walkers to make their way down
to the upstream entrance to the canyon. You are able to walk through the slot
canyon and return by a longer, but slightly less
steep track back to your starting point. But there
are dangers. The creek, hemmed in by vertical
cliffs, becomes a raging torrent following rain.
Even in fine weather large boulders triggered by
blasting at the adjacent limestone quarry (right)
can crash to the canyon floor.

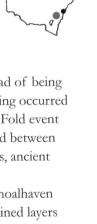

27. BURNING MOUNTAIN

You may have driven past this little gem on the New England Highway 20km north of Scone without even noticing a signpost that points to a rest area from which a track leads to the nature reserve. The big unsolved question is: who or what set the mountain alight?

When Europeans first saw the smoke they thought it was volcanic in origin.

The point of burning was then 150m to the north of its present location. From burnt rock evidence it has been determined that the coal-seam fire started near Pages River, 6km to the north. Although the rate of burning fluctuates, it has averaged slightly over 1m per year for the last century. That makes the time of ignition around 5,500 years ago. And who lit it? Suspicion falls on three possible culprits.

It may have been started by a lightning strike as the point of origin was on the surface. It may have been started by aborigines who lived in the area and almost certainly would have been aware that coal was combustible. And the third theory, and the one favoured by a number of scientists, is that it started by spontaneous combustion. No matter who or what started it; it's worth a visit. The 4.6km return trip from the rest area is along a well-made track with stairs in the few moderately steep areas. A viewing platform has been erected at the end of the track, but there are no other facilities.

Although the coal seam is 30m below the surface at the current fire front, heat radiating up from below has scorched the surface into a desolate zone of ash and burnt earth.

Sulphur deposits at smoking chimney.

Sterile ground above fire front.

28. BYADUK CAVES

The Byaduk Caves are accessed and signposted from the village of Byaduk North on the Port Fairy to Hamilton highway. The caves would be better referred to as the Byaduk Lava Tubes, because that is what they are.

The caves area is serviced by information boards and an 800m-long Byaduk Caves Discovery Walk Track. The walk passes by all four lava tubes, but only Harman One is accessible without the use of abseiling equipment. Even then, care is required as the track down into it is steep, stony and slippery. Access to the caves is restricted to summer as they are inhabited by the protected Southern

Bent-wing Bats that hibernate there in winter. Intending visitors to Harman One should wear covered shoes and carry a torch.

The lava tubes acted as conduits for the free-flowing Mount Napier lava. As the lava flowed, its surface cooled and hardened while that underneath continued flowing. When the lava stopped flowing the tubes were left empty (**#205**). Sections of roof have collapsed, exposing their existence.

Note the flatness of the surface above the tubes. The tubes vary in size and shape with the largest having a width of 18m and an internal height of 10m.

29. CABLE BEACH

Cable Beach is famous for its sand, sunsets and society; it's the right place to be seen by and with the right people. It's also an interesting

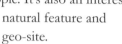

natural feature and geo-site.

Where did all the sand come from? It came from the Canning Basin, which is the second-largest geologic basin in Australia – only the Great Artesian Basin is larger. The Canning Basin covers almost half a million square kilometres of Western Australia, squeezed between the Kimberley Block and the Pilbara Craton. The basin basically filled with

sand/sandstone over a 100-million-year period commencing around 480 million years ago. Now raised, the basin supplies this part of the Western Australian coast with sand. The sand at Cable Beach has been arranged into beach and dunes by constructive waves that dominate the surf here.

Photos: Carol Moore.

Constructive waves break forward rather than straight down. Forward-breaking waves stir up little sand, but as they move forward the wave carries the bulk of its stirred-up sand far up the

beach. Once the wave has ceased its forward motion, most of the wave's water percolates down into the beach and the sand that was in motion is left stranded higher up the beach (**#84**). Wind then pushes the dry sand further inland.

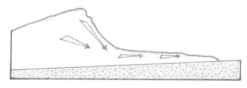

30. CADELL FAULT

The Cadell Fault was born about 70,000 years ago when earthquakes struck the usually peaceful area between what is now the New South Wales town of Deniliquin and the Victorian town of Elmore to the south of Echuca. Over the next 40,000 years, and with quakes calculated to be as high as 7.5 on the Richter Scale, land to the west of the fault was raised by 10–20m, completely blocking the Murray River and forming a large lake. The lake filled and eventually overflowed near Deniliquin. The rush of flood water released by the breach carved a new stream channel that allowed the Murray to continue flowing until it reached its old bed between Swan Hill and Mildura. The river ran along the eastern side of the fault with a high bank on its western side and virtually no bank on its other.

Photo taken from the low flat eastern bank towards the higher western bank of the Edward River near the small Riverina town of Mathura.

The Cadell Fault not only dammed the Murray – it also dammed Victoria's north-flowing Goulburn River, thus forming another lake. The Goulburn River Lake first overflowed via a low divide into the Campaspe River, but the Goulburn River too eventually cut through the Cadell Fault allowing it to flow west cutting for itself an entirely new course. This gave the Murray a choice. Either keep flowing to the north or flow south down in front of the fault until it met the Goulburn. It chose the latter.

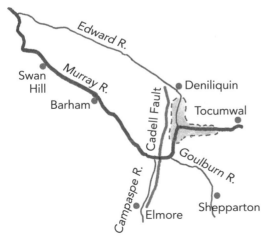

It now flows south to where it meets with the Goulburn, then west in the channel cut by the Goulburn until it eventually meets up with its original course towards Barham. The part-time Murray River that once flowed past Deniliquin is now called the Edward River and still flows when there is sufficient water in the Murray.

31. CAMOOWEAL CAVES

If you're actually expecting to get into these caves; forget it.
They are 'out of bounds' for casual visitors. And if you did
have permission and were properly equipped, you would have to
scramble down into the hole, locate the almost vertical entrance
shaft, set up your abseiling equipment, don your scuba stuff and down you go.
When you got to the bottom it may be wet or dry. The speleothems are sparse,
unspectacular and there's no coloured electric lighting. Have I put you off?

Even so, the caves are interesting and well worth a visit. To start with, the
caves are in dolomite rather than the much more common limestone. Dolomite
$[CaMg(CO_3)_2]$ is limestone with an added dash of magnesium. The splash of
magnesium makes the dolomite harder than limestone, but doesn't make it any
less resistant to attack by weak carbonic acid than its sibling. This dolomite at

Camooweal was laid down in a shallow sea around 500 million years ago. Its age is only important in that it predates the evolution of land animals. Corals weren't abundant then either, so the calcium carbonate content of the rock came primarily from decaying lime-excreting organisms and algae.

The main cave, Great Nowranie, is formed in the bed of a small non-perennial creek. Creek water has dissolved part of its bed and the underlying strata developing an underground labyrinth of cracks and caves. Dissolved cracks are exposed on the surface adjacent to the hole. Such patterned strata are termed karren (above left).

Karren can also be seen around a small sinkhole that lies between the car park and the main cave (above right). There are numerous other sinkholes in the area, but these are not visible from a distance due to the extreme flatness of this eastern extension of the Barkly Tableland. To reach the caves from Camooweal, head south from the post office along Urandangi Road for 15km and turn left at the signposted entrance. Facilities are available at nearby Nowranie Waterhole.

32. CANAL ROCKS

The rocks in Western Australia's south-west coast have had a hard life, much of it inflicted by the subcontinent of India. Granite was also injected at various times between 1,500 million–500 million years ago. India loomed on the horizon around the end of that period. Australia was then much further south than it is today with the present west coast pointing north.

India arrived by sea, first bumping into Antarctica then Australia. This initial jostle between India and Australia forced some of the granite down towards the mantle where the added heat and pressure caused the granite to reform itself as a gneiss. Gneiss, (pronounced 'niece') is crystalline and looks much like granite except it often contains dark and/or light coloured streaks.

The dark bands have concentrations of magnesium and iron while lighter bands are more quartz-like. As gneiss is being formed it may also suffer shearing forces. These forces are the same as those seen when a deck of cards is thrown on a table and individual cards slide on top of other cards. Shearing is well exposed at Canal Rocks where the stack of strata is at a slope and each stratum seriously thick.

The subsequent break-up of Gondwana, including India's rough departure, uplift, erosion and higher sea levels has now exposed the gneiss.

A boardwalk has been erected at Canal Rocks to aid scuba divers, fishers and inquisitive photographers. The slope of the rock strata is easily seen from the boardwalk.

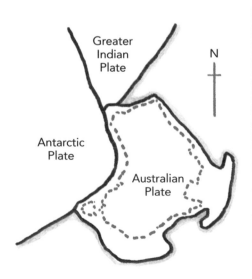

33. BASALT, TRACHYTE AND RHYOLITE

These are the most common rocks formed as lava solidifies. The three – basalt, trachyte and rhyolite – are said to be igneous, that is, they cooled and solidified from a liquid state. Meanwhile tuff (compressed volcanic ash) is sometimes thought of as being igneous and sometimes sedimentary.

All three solidified lava rocks have a common feature, poligmal (five- or six-sided) columns. These columns are caused by shrinkage within the solidifying lava as it cools. This is somewhat similar to the shrinkage of mud as it dries out.

Cracks separating columns run perpendicular to the surface from which the cooling takes place, that is, almost vertical if the lava has been free-flowing over flattish land. Cracks extend from the surface to the bottom of lava flows.

Chemically, the three rocks are different: basalt is 45–63 per cent silica (quartz) accompanied by iron and magnesium; trachyte is 60–65 per cent silica, but with more alkali feldspar than basalt; and rhyolite has around 70 per cent silica and little iron. Unless

you travel with a chemistry kit this doesn't help much in identifying the rocks, but some other characteristics will. Basalt is plain grey and due to its iron content generally breaks down to form red soils. Trachyte (left) is light

coloured and speckled. Rhyolite is also pale coloured, but if it has cooled quickly it is shiny and brittle with a common name of volcanic glass (right).

Basalt as a lava is hot (more than 1,100°C), runny (low viscosity) and may form extensive lava plains built from overlapping, thin lava flows. Trachyte and rhyolite lavas have lower temperatures (900–1,000°C), higher viscosity and build steep-sided domes as at Timor Rock (bottom left) in the Warrumbungles.

Tuff is an aggregate that may resemble cement. The example (below) has the reddish colour associated with basalt. Older and more compacted samples are quite hard.

34. CANOBOLAS'S TRACHYTE WALL

Mount Canobolas, 15km south-west of the city of Orange, is a remnant of one of eastern Australia's hot-spot volcanic chains. (**#49**)

Canobolas (below) has the classic shape of a shield volcano with low-angled flanks. When viewed from a distance it appears deceptively low, but in reality it towers more than 500m above the surrounding land.

Mount Canobolas is a 'two for the price of one' volcano. Commencing around 13 million years ago, the volcano built a smooth low profile cone with a diameter of nearly 50km. Towards the end of its life, 2 million years later, it became violent and built a series of new cones and domes that collectively stand out as pimples around the volcano. The rejuvenated volcano had a series of vents (openings) that behaved like individual volcanoes sitting on the top and flanks of the original. By the time of its demise, Canobolas had developed at least 30 of these eruptive vents.

The difference between the first and last eruptions has to do with the chemistry and temperatures of the erupted lavas. By far the greatest bulk of the original volcano, everything below the pimples, is built from hawaiite, a rock type belonging to the basalt family. Most of the lava flows were relatively thin, averaging only 2–3m in thickness. However, eruptions towards the end of the volcano's life were of trachyte and rhyolite. These types of lava are thick and tacky with lower temperatures of around 800°C and hence do not normally flow far from their eruption points before solidifying. The trachyte wall formed when trachyte oozed from an elongated vent between Young Man Canobolas and Mount Towac. The trachyte flowed only a short distance before solidifying.

35. CAPE BRIDGEWATER'S STONE FOREST

You might rightfully expect the top of Cape Bridgewater, a two- to three-million-year-old volcano, to be covered by volcanic rock, but it's not; parts are covered by calcarenite, a young and poorly cemented form of limestone.

Limestone on the adjacent sea floor was exposed during glacial maxima in the last 2.5 million years. This poorly consolidated material was blown inland to form sand hills with some of the sand covering parts of Cape Bridgewater. The 'Stone Forest' was formed within these hills.

One theory suggests that the wind-blown sand covered a forest of Moonah trees. The sand hardened around the trunks that gradually rotted away. Erosion eventually exposed the fossil forest. This sus theory of the stone forest's

origin, even though proved wrong, can be found in numerous holiday brochures. The trunks are too close to have come from a natural forest and there are no signs of roots.

Limestone surfaces that lie beneath a thin covering of soil are not always smooth. They can be dotted with solution holes as revealed in the photo of a wall section in a limestone quarry (below right). Slightly acidic water has pooled in small depressions on the limestone surface. The water has dissolved the limestone, making the depressions deeper. With repetition, the holes become deeper and filled with soil and rotting vegetation. This further speeds the process.

Water washed into the pipe-like holes may carry with it other non-limestone minerals. These minerals are deposited in the holes as the water continues to leak into the surrounding limestone. The extra minerals in the pipe walls make them harder and more resistant to erosion than the surrounding rock.

36. CAPE HILLSBOROUGH VOLCANO

In itself, Cape Hillsborough is nothing remarkable; just the scattered remnants of an old volcano sitting on the side of a quiet Queensland beach just north of MacKay. But historically, Cape Hillsborough is very important. It marks the start of

the world's longest continental hot-spot chain of volcanoes (**#49**). Although our longest chain, it's one of our youngest and only began firing at Cape Hillsborough 33 million years ago.

Things have changed a lot since then. The Cape Hillsborough Volcano at that time was away from the coast and close to a freshwater lake. Its last lava flows were of trachyte and rhyolite. When erupted, these two lavas are thick with the consistency of plastacine. They cool rapidly, solidify, and clog-up their outlets. The whole area must have been dotted with outlets only kilometres apart. As you drive towards the national park your first close view of a volcanic outlet is Pinnacle Rock (opposite below), which is a trachyte plug. Other larger rounded hills you have already passed on the way in are volcanic domes.

The beach at Cape Hillsborough appears dirty, but it's not. The bulk of the sand is from common quartz crystals derived from granites and sandstones, but here the volcano has added its own contribution; mica. One of the chemical differences between basalt and rhyolite is that rhyolite commonly contains mica. These black/grey platy crystals intermingle with the quartz sand to give the beach its 'dirty' appearance. In the right light, mica is reflective and can give the beach a shiny appearance.

37. CARLO SANDBLOW

The Carlo Sandblow is similar to comparable landforms on
Fraser Island, but is easier and cheaper to get to than those on
the island. Just drive to the town of Rainbow Beach, park and
walk. Although the Carlo Sandblow opens back from Rainbow
Beach (**#175**) both are separate landforms and their entries are by different tracks.
Ask at the tourist information office for directions to the Sandblow car park.

The sand in the coloured cliffs is quite old when compared with the age of
sand found in most beach dunes. At various times these sands have been immersed
beneath the sea. At other times, during glacial peaks, they have stood high and
dry. Fine clays have been added to the mix and over the last 500,000 years the
seesawing effects of sea-level change have led to the sorting of material based
on grain sizes. Finer grains, particularly clays, have found their way to the surface.
These grains hold the cliff face together.

Dominant south-easterly trade winds blow loose sand from the beach up and
over the ancient stabilised coloured sand dunes to form a long, partly vegetated
dune running parallel to the beach. The sandblow exists where the accumulation
of sand has been sufficiently rapid to cover existing vegetation. The same trade
winds blow sand grains across the sandblow until they reach the western side of
the dune where they tumble over the edge forming a steep lee slope to encroach
on and eventually cover the trees below. This slope creates an enticing play area for
young children, but great care is needed and children should be closely supervised.
The sand is unstable and when disturbed can form avalanches that rush down the
steep slope burying whatever lies in their path.

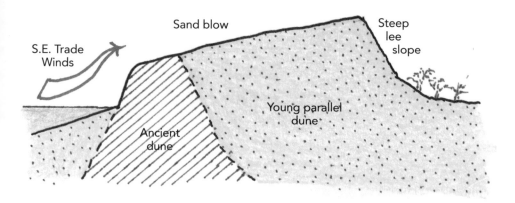

38. CARNARVON GORGE

Carnarvon Gorge lies within a national park on the Buckland Tableland that straddles the Great Dividing Range. Rivers in the western section of the park flow into the Murray-Darling system, while Carnarvon Creek drains east through the Fitzroy system to the Pacific Ocean near Rockhampton.

Back 225 million years ago this area was a shallow sea where sand was deposited. The resulting sandstone has a slight pinkish colour, but is not visible

in the gorge (right, photo taken below gorge). Carnarvon Gorge has been cut into the younger deposits that lie above. Commencing about 190 million years ago and lasting 55 million years, another depositional period built a series of near-white sandstone layers (below right) on top of the earlier sandstone and shale. This layer has the appropriate name of 'Precipice Sandstone' and is the one that forms the gorge's walls.

Separating the first and second sandstone deposits is a layer of impervious shale. Thin layers of shale are also found interbedded within the Precipice Sandstone layers. A third series, that lies above the

other two, followed. This last series is younger, less well consolidated, and more easily eroded than the earlier two. The area was uplifted around 80 million years ago at the time of the raising of the Great Dividing Range.

During the uplift many joints (vertical cracks) formed in the sandstone, but the layers remained close to horizontal in the area of the gorge. From 32 million to 27 million years ago volcanic activity in the region covered the sandstones with layers of basalt up to 300m thick.

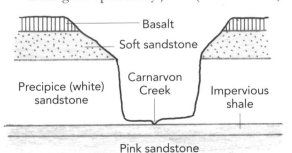

Basalt
Soft sandstone
Precipice (white) sandstone
Carnarvon Creek
Impervious shale
Pink sandstone

39. CARNARVON GORGE WALK

Following the cessation of volcanic activity, Carnarvon Creek
eroded its course, first through the basalt and then into the
sandstone below. Precipice Sandstone is particularly susceptible
to river erosion. This is because it consists of lightly cemented
individual grains of sand. Gravel and stones carried by Carnarvon Creek bounced
along the bottom chipping these grains from the bedrock, and in so doing,
progressively lowered the bed of the stream. A look at the bed of Carnarvon
Creek will confirm that the stream, when in flood, has ample ammunition for this
abrading process.

A motor vehicle is necessary to get to Carnarvon Gorge, but once there, the
only way to view this picturesque gorge is on foot. The main gorge return walk to
Cathedral Cave and back to Park Headquarters is not far short of 20km. Although
long, the track is well made and reasonably flat. Recent flooding has caused the
first sections of the track to be realigned away from the river. Once back on the

river it follows the creek all the way, crisscrossing the stream about 12 times between the end of the realigned section and Cathedral Cave. Each crossing is signposted and numbered.

Significant side tracks lead to tributary gorges and features of interest. Notable among these are: the Moss Gardens (centre right) between crossings 7 and 8 and the Amphitheatre (below right) between crossings 9 and 10. The old crossings 2 to 6 no longer exist, but the old numbering remains for the upper section. These side canyons are of special interest in that river erosion is more obvious here than along the main gorge. The short sharp bends in these canyons are the result of their streams following the paths of least resistance when cutting down; that is, following the main joint lines. Good examples can also be found of potholing where boulders, trapped in stream-bed depressions, swirl around with the water flow, deepening and broadening the depressions to form steep sided cylindrical holes. The remains of higher previous potholes can often be seen on the canyon walls. Polished rock can be seen both at the top and at the bottom ends of many pools.

40. CATARACT GORGE

Cataract Gorge has been eroded through Tasmania's extensive dolerite intrusion (**#12**). The dolerite and the gorge are direct results of the Gondwana break-up. It was a close call. A few more savage earthquakes and if the glue that keeps Tasmania attached to the mainland had not held, our island state may well have sailed off with Antarctica to a chillier neighbourhood.

Cataract Gorge lies on one of the many faults associated with the formation of the Tamar Graben around 60 million years ago. A graben, or rift valley, is a long thin valley forced or pulled down between parallel fault lines. The Tamar graben is aligned north-west to south-east. Aligned at right angles to it, is another set of faults that cross the graben. The South Esk River, home of the Cataract Gorge, joins its northern namesake at Launceston to form the Tamar. The Tamar River at present is really not a river; it's an estuary.

The gorge follows the minor south-west to north-east Cataract Fault. The steep sides of the 5km-long Cataract Gorge are due to the vertical cracks that developed in the dolerite as it cooled from a molten state. When a column erodes and falls it exposes another column that is equally vertical, so that erosion sees a retreat of the banks, but no change in their slopes.

The basins in the gorge have formed where other faults cross the Cataract

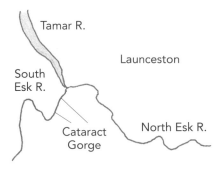

Fault, creating shatter zones that the river has vigorously eroded to form wide deep holes. The First Basin (bottom), to which most people drive, is a great example of a shatter zone. The Cataract Fault cuts through the basin from the basin's top to bottom. However, another fault runs at right angles to the Cataract Fault from the top car park down the gentle valley, across the pool and continues along Snake Gully. Frequent movement over millions of years along this fault and the Cataract Fault caused the pulverisation of the rocks at their junction. The small size of Snake and Carpark Gullies is the result of their small drainage basins and meagre water flow, rather than indicating the size of the fault. Flood waters raging down Cataract Gorge have scoured out the basin to its current maximum depth of 36m.

Track along Cataract Gorge.

41. CHANNEL COUNTRY

The Channel Country lies mainly in south-west Queensland but spills over into New South Wales, South Australia and the Northern Territory. Driving across this plain is like driving on a near-flat sea with almost imperceptible gentle low swells 5–20km apart.

About 100 million years ago the Channel Country was covered by a shallow sea extending south from the present Gulf of Carpentaria. Streams from the east, south and west poured sediment into the sea. The climate was moist at this time and continued to be so until around 30 million years ago.

Around 60 million years ago the separation of Australia and Antarctica led to a rebalancing of the Australian Continent. Although the Channel Country was nowhere near the break-up line, the upheaval did allow this section of the continent to rise, and become dry land. Sedimentation continued with flooding forming vast alluvial plains the size of some European countries. Channel Country deposits became tens of metres deep.

As the climate warmed and dried, river flows dwindled. Gradients in the river channels now average around 1cm per kilometre and water flow is so sluggish that only suspended clay particles are moved. When the streams flood they spread out over the surrounding country forming slow-moving lakes tens of kilometres wide. These lakes eventually lose their water by evaporation and/or seepage. As the surface water disappears, clay particles are deposited on the surface of the plain or are carried down into the soil by seepage. The upper 2–5m of the surface is now an almost impermeable layer of fine sand and clay. Only after major flooding do streams flow on to reach the usually dry Lake Eyre. Each stream consists of numerous channels that divide and redivide.

The Channel Country. Photo: Ian Boxall.

42. CHEVRON ROCK

Chevron Rock is one of the contorted rock formations within the Narooma Accretionary Complex. Around 450 million years ago a section of ocean floor was scraped off the ocean crustal plate as it subducted beneath Australia and tacked onto what was to become the south coast of New South Wales. Fragments of that accretion (add-ons) may be viewed along the coast from Murramarang to Narooma, New South Wales, and at Quarry Beach in Mallacoota, Victoria. Most of the complex's eye-grabbing sites are associated with the Wagona Group of rocks.

The rocks within the Wagona Group include chert, slate and turbidites. Chert is related to flint, slate is compressed and metamorphosed mudstone, and turbidites are layers of rock formed from undersea landslides. The collision between the ocean crust and the continent saw many of the accretionary rocks forced deep towards the Earth's mantle before being raised again towards the surface.

The power of this scrunching is best illustrated at Chevron Rock. The chevrons are zigzag folds formed under extreme heat and pressure.

To get there follow Glasshouse Rocks Road to the Narooma Cemetery; turn right (south) just before you enter the cemetery and park at the end of the road. A track leads south along a short section of cemetery fence then continues into the trees. The main track divides a number of times. Keep going left and always down. It's a bit rough, so take care. Mark where you come out, as it's not that easy to find the track on the way back.

43. CHILLAGOE MARBLE

Your best view of Chillagoe marble is on the way into town from
the south where abandoned quarries are located on both sides of the
roadwat and discarded blocks lie nearby (bottom). Chillagoe lies on
the edge of Queensland's most extensive limestone belt. This limestone is about
400 million years old and dates from when the area lay below sea level.

But it's not as simple as that. If you visit
Chillagoe's Information Centre you will find
the geologic history of the area clearly laid out
before you on a series of info boards. They tell
the stories of underwater volcanoes, continents
bumping together and then separating more
than a few times, intrusions of granite, the
arrival of copper, tin, zinc, gold, iron and other
minerals, and the conversion of some of the
limestone into marble. The marble was created by the intrusion of granite and
volcanic rocks into the limestone. By then the limestone had already been upended.
The heat given off by the intruding granite and volcanics as they cooled, baked the
limestone altering its structure and changing it into marble.

A ridge of marble (above) can be viewed at the garbage dump off the road to
the smelter site, and also at a working quarry adjacent to the old smelter.

Marble is much smoother than limestone and exhibits fewer of limestone's
rills and flutes. This is because of marble's tighter crystal structure and its
imperviousness. However, over time, marble, like limestone, slowly dissolves under
contact with weak carbonic acid and will develop caves and speleothems.

The caves, also at Chillagoe, are in limestone that was away from the granite
and the volcanics.

44. CHINA WALL

China Wall is up to 6m high and runs for around 15km, with its top disappearing below the surface in places. It's only 6km from Halls Creek with free access through private property.

China Wall is an interesting quartz dyke. There are thousands of quartz dykes in Australia (but none as spectacular as this one) and all have been formed in the same way. Superheated water trapped below the surface and containing dissolved silicon and oxygen has been forced at great pressure towards the surface through a crack, joint line, or fault. The openings have widened, lessening the pressure and lowering the temperature to a point where the silicon has precipitated as crystals of silicon dioxide (SiO_2), quartz. As more and more water rose to replace the escaping water, precipitation continued until the gap was eventually filled. As the new rock mass cooled, it contracted, forming a pattern of brick wall-like cracks. After the surface above the dyke was eroded away, the dyke was exposed. Quartz is much more resistant to erosion than most other rocks.

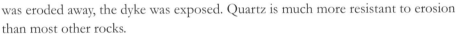

The dyke appears to stop abruptly at the creek just beneath the main viewing point. But this is not so. The creek at this point is following along a fault. This is not an ordinary fault where rock on one side is raised or lowered in relation to the other; this is a lateral fault. With lateral faults, rock and land on one side of the fault slides sideways in relation to the rock and land on the other side.

The land opposite the viewing area and containing the wall has slid a couple of hundred metres to the left in relation to the raised section on which the viewing area is located. If you walk to the right from the viewing point, the quartz wall will appear again on your side of the creek. But please do not do this, as requested by the owners. You can view that part of the wall on your left as you drive out.

45. CLONCURRY TO MOUNT ISA

Cloncurry to Mount Isa is extensive for a geo-site, but one of the most interesting short drives in Queensland. The road surface is excellent and the grades reasonable. Unfortunately it is used extensively by ore-carrying road-trains. They probably won't hold you up, but a hundred tonnes of truck and ore doesn't stop very quickly. It's a safety problem.

The rocks in the hills here are ancient. They form part of the North Australian Craton that dates back nearly 2 billion years (**#7**). The area around Mount Isa and Cloncurry was stretched and compressed numerous times in the next billion years. Granite was intruded in the middle of these times and also towards its end. At the same time, quartz and other minerals were added. Even the usually silky smooth quartz was broken and shattered. Evidence of compression slippage within quartz can be seen in the close-up photo (above left).

Older sedimentaries were pressured and formed into hard metamorphic rocks. Erosion removed the least resistant rocks leaving only the toughest for you to look at. They stick up at odd angles with some looking as if they have been squeezed from a giant toothpaste-like tube lying beneath the surface.

The Mount Isa Geological Province is claimed to contain 21 per cent of the world's lead, 11 per cent of its zinc, 5 per cent of its silver and nearly 2 per cent of its copper. It also produces large quantities of gold as a by-product in the refining the other metals. That makes it one of the world's most significant sources of economic minerals.

Left: Just east of Mount Isa.

Opposite: Spectacular peak adjacent to Cloncurry town campground.

46. COBBOLD GORGE

If you like peace, quietness and a close look at nature, this is just the spot. The spectacular hidden gorge lies in a family-owned cattle station/low impact tourist development in northern Queensland south of Georgetown.

The geological history of the gorge is contentious. Some suggest that the 10,000-year-old gorge is the result of river capture. In a science that usually talks in hundreds of millions of years, ten thousand is equal to this morning. About 1.5km upstream from where the present-day Cobbold Creek joins the Robertson River is a dry river valley. This hints that this dry valley is the original course of Cobbold Creek. Some suggest that a lower level creek eroded upstream until its headwaters cut into Cobbold Creek. This diverted its flow leaving the downstream section of the 'original' Cobbold Creek starved of water. With a much greater flow of water diverted from the original Cobbold Creek, the 'new' Cobbold Creek has cut the present day narrow gorge.

Another solution is that the area around the gorge and the Robertson River has an ancient as well as modern history of faulting and uplift. A moderate uplift of around 1m could have caused the old creek to become dammed and overflow, diverting to a new channel across the sandstone and into what was then a smaller and pre-existing gully. The new section of creek cut down into and along a joint line into the 50m-thick layer of sandstone creating the present gorge. It's your choice as to which explanation you accept.

Supporters of both would agree that the main eroding process here would have been potholing. Potholing occurs when boulders trapped in stream-bed depressions are swirled around by the running water. This results in the boulders being worn-down and the size of the depressions increased. As the holes become larger they trap more and larger boulders that continue the eroding process. The holes eventually coalesce as the process is repeated over and over. Polished abandoned potholes are clearly visible in the sides of the gorge.

The gorge can only be visited by guided tour from the Cobbold Gorge Resort and Campground. Exploring the gorge is undertaken in electric, flat-bottomed boats.

47. COOBER PEDY OPAL

There's a recipe for making opal: 1. Dissolve silica (quartz sand) in acid; 2. Neutralise the acid; 3. Evaporate the liquid so that the dissolved silica precipitates onto a hard surface. Yes, they do actually make synthetic opal. It's a little more complex than as outlined above and the quality's not all that great, but it is done.

Over a longish period of time parts of Australia followed the same recipe. It did it so well that Australia now supplies more than 90 per cent of the world's opal. Back between 120 million and 90 million years ago much of inland of Australia was covered by the shallow Eromanga Sea that extended over most of what is now the Great Artesian Basin and more. The climate was equatorial and luxuriant forests grew along the sea's edges. With the decay of vegetation came the release of humic acid and an increase in ground water acidity. The acid was weak, but it had 30 million years to dissolve some of the silicon in its surrounding sand. Step No 1 was accomplished, but there was no opal.

From 90 million years ago, seas fell, the Eromanga Sea dried up and it was back to dry land again. But the climate was still warm and moist and forests dominated. With surface water gone, iron oxide was carried down and accumulated in the first layer of sandstone it encountered. Still no opal.

Between 35 million and 30 million years ago massive climate changes occurred. The central Australian deserts formed and soil water movement changed from down seepage to loss by evaporation. Leftover ocean salt was carried back to the surface and accumulated as salt pans. But still no opal.

That all began to change around 25 million years ago, following some tectonic (crustal) movements. Much of the old Eromanga surface was forced into gentle waves like giant ocean swells with the crests generally 2–50km apart and wave heights (from trough to crest) of from 20–200m. It was only after the formation of these gentle anticlines and synclines (upfolds and downfolds) that opal formation commenced.

Opal is associated with the crests of the anticlines. Although slopes were very gentle, often less than 1:100, ground water containing small quantities of dissolved silica slowly moved down and away from the crests. This path was followed each time it rained. The water dried out 20–30m below the surface and the silica deposited in small non-continuous cavities. Repetition led to more deposition and increased thickness to the opal deposit.

If viewed under a powerful microscope, opal can be seen to consist of millions of tiny blue spheres laid in rows like oranges packed for display at a fruit market. The larger the spheres, and the more consistent their size, the better the quality of opal. Small and disorganised spheres produce white or colourless opal termed potch (above). Thin flakes of coloured opal are often glued to potch to enhance their colour and to strengthen the stone.

48. COORONG

Goolwa

L. Alexandrina

Murray R.

Murray Mouth

L. Albert

Younghusband Peninsula

The Coorong

5km

The Coorong is part of the Murray River Delta that has been formed from both local and distant suppliers of sand. Victor Harbour Granite just to the west is the local supplier with its sand moved to the Coorong by ocean currents, while Kosciuszko Granite, the distant supplier, has had its sand transported by the Murray River and its tributaries.

During the last ice age, the Murray River was fed by melting glaciers and/or snow that covered most of the Monaro and Southern Alps. The river was also longer. Sea level was around 130m lower than at present and the mouth of the Murray was tens of kilometres further south, at the edge of the continental shelf. With the change of climate at the end of the age, temperatures and sea level both rose and the lower Murray River was drowned and entered the ocean in the Lake Alexandrina Gulf. During flood time, the river continued to carry large quantities of sand beyond its mouth and into the ocean. The sand was dropped where flow ceased. This accumulation of sand quickly built to a point where it formed islands that blocked the gulf creating Lakes Alexandrina

and Albert. The Murray then flowed to the sea between the islands. The western river mouth eventually dominated as sand gradually blocked the Lake Albert mouth.

At the same time, east-flowing currents carried Victor Harbour sand along the coast to add to the growing barrier in a similar manner to that of the Gippsland Lakes in Victoria (**#159**). This barrier, the Younghusband Peninsula, has created a 150km-long beach backed by a long thin lake, the Coorong. The top of the barrier consists of poorly stabilised dunes. Those dunes facing the ocean are much steeper and more mobile than those facing the Coorong.

The construction of weirs to assist navigation along the Murray, and dams to aid irrigation and provide water supply, have vastly changed the river's natural flow. In addition, the construction of barrages across the Murray at Goolwa and between Lake Alexandrina and the Coorong in the 1930s has reduced the natural flow of brackish water into and out of the lakes system.

49. COSGROVE VOLCANO CHAIN

The world's longest continental hot-spot chain was
identified by a team of ANU researchers in 2015.
Hot-spots are places on the Earth's crust where
plumes of heat rising from near Earth's core reach
the base of the solid crust and form reservoirs of
molten magma. If that magma melts through to the
surface, a hot-spot volcano results. If the hot-spot
lasts for millions of years and the crust moves over
the hot-spot, a chain of volcanoes will form
a line running in the opposite direction to the
crustal movement. This movement is best illustrated
by making a pencil mark on a loose sheet of paper;
then moving the paper in one direction while at the same
time, making more marks with the pencil held in its original position. The marks
will line up in the opposite direction to the direction the paper is being pulled.

Cape Hillsborough 33 mya
Nebo 32 mya
Peak Range 30 mya
Springsure 28 mya
Buckland 25 mya

Byrock 17 mya
El Capitan 17 mya
Lake Cargelligo 15 mya

Cosgrove 9 mya

Australia is moving northwards at around 6–8cm per year. The Cosgrove chain
of volcanoes (location and ages on map) first broke through the crust 33 million
years ago at Cape Hillsborough (**#36**) on the central coast of Queensland.
Fortunately for history, the volcano's last dying gasp eruption was of rhyolite,
a lava that forms rock much more resistant to erosion than the more easily eroded
common basalt.

Four volcanoes – Byrock, El Capitan, Cargelligo and Cosgrove – had previously
been classified as belonging to a separate track. They were different to other
Australian volcanoes in that their basalts contained the mineral leucite.

The ANU team proved that leucite was present at these sites only because the
lithosphere (rocky crust plus non-fluid part of the upper mantle) was thicker there
than 130km. They found that leucite can only be absorbed by magma to form
leucitite at pressures greater than those exerted by lithospheric depths greater than
130km. The ANU team went on to prove that the leucitite volcanoes were an
extension of the Hillsborough-Buckland hot-spot track. This extended track has a
length of over 2,000km – by far the longest continental based track in the world.
Minor earthquake activity indicates that the present location of the Cosgrove
hot-spot plume now lies in Bass Strait off the north-west coast of Tasmania.
It is thought that the hot-spot is gradually losing its puff.

Cape Hillsborough Volcano.

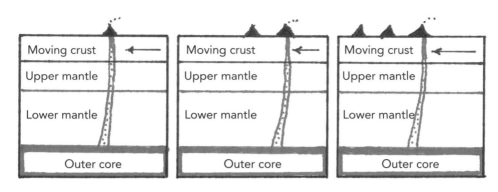

50. CRADLE MOUNTAIN

Two of the most photographed natural features in Tasmania,
Cradle Mountain and Dove Lake are truly deserving of their
popularity. Peaceful, evocative, tranquil and serene are words used to describe
the scenery. If you are bold enough to climb into the cradle, words such as
exhilarating, daunting, grand and awe-inspiring may be more appropriate. Well,
that's all the promotional adjectives used up! Let's look at the rocks and some of
the region's glacial shapes.

Cradle Mountain has been shaped by the interaction of ancient geology with
recent scouring by glaciers. Like much of Tasmania, the geology is dominated
by quartzite, sandstone and dolerite (**#12**). At Cradle Mountain the once upper
level of sandstone has been completely removed by erosion along with most
of the dolerite. A close look at the photos (opposite above and below) reveals
a cliff on the horizon at the foot of the left-hand peak (Little Horn). This cliff
is conglomerate, a member of the sandstone family group, while above it are
the near-vertical and broken columns of dolerite which form the twin peaks

and the cradle. Beneath the conglomerate and below the right-hand peaks in the photograph above, the bare face of extremely hard and ancient quartzite is obvious. At the glacial extreme, the surface level of the ice was probably around the quartzite-sandstone interface.

The large Rodway Glacier, on the southern side and parallel to the Cradle Peaks line, flowed past the ridge scouring out a steep-sided U-shaped valley. On the northern side of that same line, the Dove Creek Glacial Cirque cut back into the Cradle Peaks ridge forming a sharp arête. An arête is often referred to as a serrate ridge, and the gap between peaks as a col.

The long ridge line of Little Horn (1,355m), the Cradle, Weindorfers Tower, (1,459m) and Cradle Mountain (1,545m) stood out above the ice.

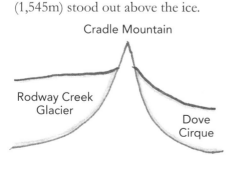

Cradle Mountain

Rodway Creek Glacier

Dove Cirque

51. CUTTA CUTTA CAVES

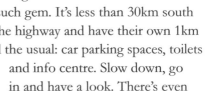

People go hurtling down the Stuart Highway between the tourist hot-spots of Darwin, Kakadu, Katherine Gorge and Alice Springs without even considering that there may be little gems in between and along the way. Cutta Cutta Caves is one such gem. It's less than 30km south of Katherine. The caves are signposted off the highway and have their own 1km sealed entrance road. At the road's end are all the usual: car parking spaces, toilets

and info centre. Slow down, go in and have a look. There's even a bonus; once in the nature park's developed area you have access to two excellent above-ground walks, the Karst Walk and the Woodland Walk.

The caves are uncommon in a number of ways. They are the only limestone caves in the Northern Territory that are open to the public; they are shallow, only about 15m below the surface, and they flood annually. The flooding occurs during the wet season and affects the general colouration within the caves. Some speleothems have a split personality; one part stained brown and other part sparkling white. Glistening white is a sign of active growth on a speleothem while various shades of brown indicate little or no growth in recent times.

The Tindall Limestone in which the caves are located began forming 570 million years ago, but it took another 200 million years to pass before the land was uplifted and the caves commenced to form.

Cutta Cutta Caves have the full gamut of common limestone formations: stalactites, stalagmites, straws, columns, shawls and flow stones, all shaped by water flow, calcite formation rates and chance (**#1**). One broken column in the cave (below right) is said to be evidence of a World War 2 soldier having used it for target practice. Note the white tips that indicate that healing is occurring. A couple more thousand years and it may be totally restored.

At the time of writing (2020), commercial tours of the caves operate on the hour from April to November. Above-ground tours of the karst area are free.

52. DARLING DOWNS' BLACK SOIL

Soil scientists refer to the world's best examples of black soils as chernozems (Russian for 'black soil'), as found on the Russian steppe and the North American prairie. The Darling Downs' soils are not true chernozems; let's just say they're close relatives. The chernozem family characteristics of blackness, high humus and clay content, and a dominance of grass are all on show on the downs.

'Down' is a quaint Old English term used to describe a region of gentle hills formed on a foundation of chalk. Early English settlers found little or no chalk in their new colony, but still used the term loosely to describe any area of gently undulating land. The Darling Downs may not have chalk, but they do have the one unifying physical factor; black clay soil.

The black colour is due to the region's climate and its responding vegetation. It's hot in summer, but coolish in winter with some frosts. Most rain falls in summer, but in winter there's enough to keep plants alive. The Darling Downs experience extreme variability in weather and climatic conditions including high evaporation rates and savage droughts.

December average rainfall is around 95mm, but in 2016 the potential evaporation rate was in excess of 300mm. Potential evaporation is the amount of evaporation that would take place if the water was available.

Plants have problems with these numbers. In the eastern Downs where rainfall is higher, trees happily grow, but struggle in drought years. To the west where rainfall is lower, trees grow further apart or even move out and leave it to the grasses. And it's the grasses that are really important. They grow tall and leafy. When the annuals die, or the perennials go into their version of hibernation, they shed vast quantities of leaves. These leaves do not completely rot away; that which

remains is termed humus and becomes incorporated in the soil. Black humus makes up 10–15 per cent of the Darling Downs' topsoil, and if you add 10 per cent of black to most anything, that anything becomes dark. Humus adds both fertility and water-holding capacity to the soil.

53. DEAKIN ANTICLINAL RIDGES

Nearly all the hills in Canberra are of volcanic origin, but on the southern side of the Deakin shops, near the sporting fields, a shale anticline (upfold) is exposed. Part of the anticlinal fold was quarried to obtain shale for brick making in Canberra's early history. An information board giving the geologic history of the area and a map of a short walking track around the site has been erected. Walk the track. You can see the folds in the rocks and come to understand how the bending has caused the shale layers to break.

Just over 400 million years ago what is now Canberra was a shallow sea and home to numerous volcanoes. Some volcanic sediments, along with fine sandstone, limestone and shale, were deposited in the sea. Later compression saw some of these sediments squeezed into gentle folds. A shallow valley separates the two exposed ridges. The southernmost of the two (right in photo below right) is the younger rock as it once (before erosion and quarrying) lay over and above the Deakin-side ridge.

Shale (below left) is an interesting rock. It is fine textured and comprised of clay and silt particles. An exposed section on the top of the main ridge shows how shale weathers into small thin platelets that can be blown or washed away. Pick up a platelet. It is easily broken between your fingers.

54. DERBY'S MUDFLATS

The area around Derby is in the perfect location for the
development of mudflats. King Sound, on which the mudflats have
formed, is protected from storm waves by the string of islands that
form the Buccaneer Archipelago. The sound is the mouth for the Fitzroy River,
which is Australia's largest river by volume of flow. The Fitzroy is also the source
of fine silt and mud that the massive tides have rearranged to build the flats. Derby
is on the eastern side of the Sound and approximately 30km north of the Fitzroy's
mouth.

The slope of the mudflats and the adjacent King Sound floor is around 1°.
Within the flats, tidal channels have developed with each channel experiencing
a regular tidal pattern with strong shoreward flow on the rising tide and a
corresponding outward flow on the ebb. The flats have been built up by sediments
washed in by rising tides rather than by deposits from nearby local land surface
run-off. Low levee banks occasionally develop along the edges of these channels.

Mangroves grow at the back of the flats, but find it impossible to grow further
down slope. This is because these tree cannot survive total immersion. The
mangroves that do grow are so far back that only the last 1.5–2m of the highest
tides actually reach them.

Photo: Yvonne Barrett.

55. GRANITE

Granite has much in common with grandma's fruitcake. It has a few basic ingredients together with lots of other lesser components that can be varied or left out; has many different recipes, and takes a long time to cook. Granite's basic ingredients are quartz, feldspar and mica. Quartz is usually clear but can be cloudy white through to dark grey. Feldspars also come in a variety of colours ranging through white and pale cream to grey or pink. Mica's thin shiny flakes can be light or dark. It's not the colour that makes granite recognisable, it is its texture; it's like a fruitcake.

Granite is at the core of all continents. It is the core because it is the least dense (lightest) of the igneous rocks and tends to 'float' on other igneous rocks such as basalt. Igneous rocks are those that solidify from a molten state. Basalt forms a rocky floor to the great oceans while granite, along with sedimentaries, comprise the bulk of continents. The specific gravity (weight) of water is $1g/cm^3$; for granite it is $2.6–2.7g/cm^3$ and for basalt $2.8–3.0g/cm^3$.

Granite begins life as a rising molten blob of rock that doesn't reach the surface. This because it is denser (heavier) than the rock above it, but less dense (lighter) than that below. In this equilibrium position it takes millions of years to progress through the cooling, crystallising and solidifying stages. All this while it's buried 2–12km below the surface. You don't get to see granite on the surface until erosion has removed all that overlying rock. So, by the time you see it, it's already old.

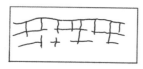

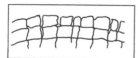

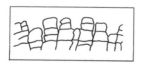

When granite is first exposed, and even before that, it starts to crack. Why? As the overlying rock is eroded away it lessens the pressure on the granite. When the pressure is reduced, the granite's response is to expand. But how? Granite doesn't expand very well. It cracks!

Stage 1 The granite's reaction to the release of pressure is for the upper layers to expand upwards and outwards forming a pattern of fine cracks both parallel and vertical to the surface.

Stage 2 Water and air penetrate the cracks. Vegetation roots follow the water and air. Exposed surfaces of the granite begin to weather (disintegrate).

Stage 3 The release of internal pressure within each block causes further fracturing with some boulders

splitting in half again and again. Some exposed surface blocks completely disintegrate and are eroded away.

Stage 4 The top layer is completely removed. These processes can then be repeated over and over for millions or billions of years.

This process is termed rock pressure reduction and applies to all bodies of granite found all over the world. Granite at or near the surface always has a pattern of horizontal and vertical cracks. It's just like the original Rubik's Cube, but without the colours or the capacity to be manipulated.

56. DEVILS MARBLES

Some worry about the long-term future for our iconic natural features such as the Great Barrier Reef and our tropical rainforests, but there's no such concern for the Devils Marbles. They're going to be with us forever. Well, almost! They're granite; and what's beneath them? More granite. And beneath that, more and more of the same.

Granite is an igneous rock that, when exposed, weathers and erodes to form distinctive shapes. Devils Marbles is Australia's most iconic example of a granitic landscape. The marbles are around 1,600 million years old and over that time erosion has removed 8km or more of overlying rock. One doesn't know how many cycles the Devils Marbles have already passed through since first being exposed. As the rocks you see now slowly disintegrate and erode, underneath a new version is feverishly being prepared (perhaps 'feverishly' is something of an overstatement).

The 'Marbles' have textbook examples of granite fracturing under a combination of shrinkage and the development of both horizontal and vertical joints.

Prismatic blocks have been rounded by spheroidal weathering. This process is often referred to as 'onion skin' weathering, as large platy sections of the surface rock become loose and slide off in much the same manner as an onion can be reduced in size by removing one layer at a time.

The separation of the outermost layer is thought to be from the rhythm of

diurnal temperature change. Around sunrise, temperatures on the rock surface rise, especially if that surface is facing the sun. The surface expands, but the inner rock is slow to heat, thus causing tension to develop between the two. This condition continues through to the evening when air temperatures fall. Under these conditions the surface contracts pulling tight on the rock core beneath that is slow to shed its heat. This daily tug-a-war eventually causes separation of the two. The clear desert skies at the marbles makes for large diurnal (daily) ranges in temperatures that accentuate the rates of exfoliation.

57. DIAMOND HEAD

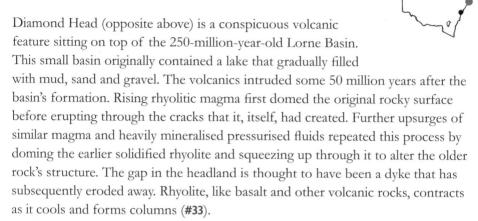

Diamond Head (opposite above) is a conspicuous volcanic
feature sitting on top of the 250-million-year-old Lorne Basin.
This small basin originally contained a lake that gradually filled
with mud, sand and gravel. The volcanics intruded some 50 million years after the
basin's formation. Rising rhyolitic magma first domed the original rocky surface
before erupting through the cracks that it, itself, had created. Further upsurges of
similar magma and heavily mineralised pressurised fluids repeated this process by
doming the earlier solidified rhyolite and squeezing up through it to alter the older
rock's structure. The gap in the headland is thought to have been a dyke that has
subsequently eroded away. Rhyolite, like basalt and other volcanic rocks, contracts
as it cools and forms columns (**#33**).

The tops of these columns are clearly visible on the wave-cut platform on the
head's north side. What is more eye-catching, however, is the platform's bright
yellow colour. Rhyolite is usually pale grey. At Diamond Head both colours
are found. Note the grey colour of the rhyolite rocks behind the beach in the
background of the photograph (below left).

Mineralised fluids are the villains of this landscape. Prior to the eruptions, the
rock had been forced down to near the mantle where it melted. As the Proto-
Pacific Plate plunged beneath the growing Australian Plate the marine plate carried
with it huge quantities of water. The locked-in water could not burst into steam,
but at such high temperatures it dissolved large quantities of silicon and oxygen
(SiO_2, that is, quartz), iron pyrite (FeS_2, fool's gold), a little real gold and copper,
plus other minerals. The dissolved Iron pyrite broke down to iron and sulphuric
acid. The iron and acid mix played havoc with the rhyolite, altering some minerals
to give the rhyolite adjacent to Diamond Head its yellow colour.

The dissolved silicon oxide has the naming rights to the headland.
It precipitated to form near-perfect crystals of clear quartz that sparkle in

sunlight. Best samples are found near
old gold mining sites near the top of the
plateau. Samples can be seen at the park's
information office.

Indian Head (opposite below) is located
in the same national park. The headland
has even more brilliant colours than its
sibling and even boasts a magnificent arch.

58. DINOSAUR STAMPEDE

About 95 million years ago a very ordinary thing happened.
A theropod (meat-eating dinosaur), *Tyrannosauropus*, nearly the size of
Tyrannosaurus, attacked about 150 smaller dinosaurs of two different
species feeding at the edge of a muddy lake. The smaller dinosaurs panicked and
ran, scattering in all directions. What is truly remarkable is that a miner fossicking
for opals in outback Queensland just a few years ago stumbled on the footprints.
The *Tyrannosauropus* was 8–9m long and stood 3–3.5m high. It could run on its two
huge hind legs at around 30km an hour. Each of its footprints (below) was 50cm
long and the length of its stride was 3.5m. The *Tyrannosauropus* ate other dinosaurs
for its food.

The middle-sized guys, *Wintonopus latomorum*, were ornithopods. Ornithopods
are the type of dinosaur that you might have wanted to keep as a pet. They grew
to the size of an emu and ate grass, ferns and tree leaves. They had probably
come down to the waterhole to drink. Their footprints (opposite above) are much
thinner than those of the Theropod and less than half its size. They could only
run at half the speed of the attacking *Tyrannosauropus*.

The little guys, *Skartopus australis,* were coelurosaurs, also theropods, but about the same size as a domestic chook. They ate insects, frogs, lizards, other small animals and eggs. Their footprints are only about 4–5cm long and they could run at about 12km an hour. You could probably catch one if you had been around at their time. However, as humans had not yet evolved, that's something you missed out on.

And did the *Tyrannosauropus* get its dinner? We don't know. All we can see are the 3,300 fossilised footprints. There are possibly thousands more footprints to be found, but scientists have only uncovered some of them, leaving the others hidden and protected below layers of covering sandstone.

59. DISMAL SWAMP

Have you ever seen a polje? Well here's your chance. A polje is a giant sinkhole. Sinkholes are areas of surface subsidence caused by roof collapse in caves or tunnels below. The only difference between a sinkhole and a polje is size. It's like the difference between a creek and a river. There's no definite size that separates one from the other, but as rivers are generally larger than creeks, poljes are generally larger than sinkholes. Dismal Swamp is large. It is 4km long and 1–2km in width. It is claimed to be the largest polje in the Southern Hemisphere. That may be an exaggerated claim, but I'm fairly certain that it's at least the largest in Australia.

To be termed a 'polje', a formation must have a flat floor, internal drainage and more often than not, steep sides. Polje is a Serbo-Croat word that simply means

'field'. In English, the use of polje is further restricted by the polje's location; having to be found in carboniferous (calcite, limestone, dolomite, etc.) rocks.

The Dismal Swamp Polje's position is unusual in that it runs along the crest of a tight anticline. The top layer of sandstone and conglomerate that forms the sides of the polje has been eroded away exposing the dolomite beneath. The swamp has a poorly formed rolling-pin shape, with its handles and axis running almost north-south. Running parallel to the swamp and delineating the polje's area are two steep inward-facing low ridges. The southern end, although open, has no obvious drainage line, while to the west a gap in the ridge and a low divide in the north allow for unchannelled overflow during winter. If you visit in summer you may find the swamp to be dry. It appears that internal flow passages are poorly formed or partially blocked by the swamp's floor of mixed sand, soil, clay and decaying vegetation.

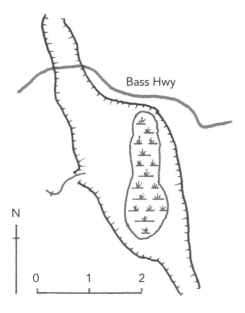

60. DOG ROCK

This faithful dog has been guarding the site of Middleton Road in Albany for more than a billion years. He's a true Top Dog and classified by the National Trust. In the local Noongar language he's *Yacka*, meaning 'wild dog tamed'.

Dog Rock has been sculptured in the usual ways for granite (**#55**). Can you see some onion-skin weathering around the jowl and beneath the brow? And is that snout the edge of a granite block? Dog Rock is well bred – his siblings include The Gap, Natural Bridge (opposite above) and many granite headlands and beaches.

The granite here is very old, even for a granite. It rose to beneath the surface following the collision between Australia and its then neighbour, Antarctica.

Photo: Ian Boxall.

61. DOVE LAKE

After looking at Cradle Mountain (**#50**), your eyes naturally travel down to Dove Lake. From above, the lake appears as a poorly drawn figure of eight. That part of Dove Lake closest to the cradle is a cirque lake while the section north of the dividing peninsula is a scour lake. The underwater contour confirms this shape with depths of 64m in the cirque and only 50m in the scour. The peninsula between the two parts is extremely resistant quartzite that forced the glacier to ride up and over it as it left the cirque and then down again into fractured rock before rising again to continue its slow down-valley movement.

Cirques form at the heads of glaciers where snow and ice accumulate. Cirques

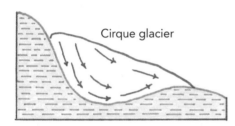

Cirque glacier

develop an armchair shape with steep back walls scoured by the down sliding movement of ice. The ice is thickest at the back of the cirque, giving it greater weight there and allowing faster movement.

Scour lakes form under the body of a glacier and indicate locations where the valley's rocky floor was broken or cracked allowing the ice to erode faster than elsewhere along its path. The flatter land around the scour section of Dove Lake formed beneath an earlier and larger continental-type glacier that crept over the edge of the plateau and overwhelmed the Dove Lake Glacier.

More as a textbook example of a cirque is the adjacent, but inappropriately named, Crater Lake (opposite below). It has that deep armchair shape and even a broad 'U' shape at the lake's exit. Lake Lilla and Wombat Pool are also cirque lakes.

For something as large as a glacier, evidence of the mechanics of its eroding power may be difficult to find. But on top of Glacier Rock and some other

exposed bare surfaces, you may find faint scratches running parallel to the direction the glacier was moving. These are striations; grooves cut into the surface of underlying rock by rocks held at the bottom of the glacier as it slid over them at rates of 1–10m a day.

62. EBOR FALLS

On the outskirts of Ebor village are the twin upper falls (below left), while a couple of hundred metres downstream lie the much taller but plainer lower falls (below right).

The twin upper falls mark where the Guy Fawkes River has cut through four separate lava flows. The near-horizontal line between the top and the next lava flow can be seen running across, halfway down and behind the top fall. The second fall runs across the third flow before dropping over it and the fourth flow, and onto a fifth flow. A similar separation line to that behind the top fall can be seen between the third and fourth flows. These upper falls have a combined height of 27m.

The Ebor Volcano, a member of a north-south hot-spot volcanic chain, has mainly eroded away. The volcano was active and grew to be quite large 18 million years ago. It is estimated to have risen 500m above the surrounding land and had a footprint some 50km in width. It flowed huge quantities of basalt with some of the flows more than 50m thick. Basalt erodes relatively quickly under the warm wet conditions that still exist in the area. (Point Lookout averages more than 150cm of rain annually.)

The volcano's core is nowhere to be seen. Its outlet is somewhere in the Upper Bellinger/Upper Macleay region called 'The Crescent'. It's off the end of Point Lookout. Its precise location, now under dense rainforest, has never been identified.

The 63m lower falls tumble over another series of lava flows. These lower falls lack the symmetry of the upper falls as the lava flows at this point were not horizontal.

63. EDGE OF THE WORLD

The plaque reads:

THE EDGE OF THE WORLD
I cast my pebble onto the shore of Eternity,
To be washed by the Ocean of Time.
It has shape, form and substance.
It is me.
One day I will be no more.
But my pebble will remain here.
On the shore of Eternity.
Mute witness for the aeons.
That today I came and stood.
At the edge of the world.

Brian Inder

Are these great words of wisdom? Do they tell you something? Is it a nonsense statement? I don't know. What I do know is that it draws people in droves to the Edge of the World, which happens to be at the mouth of the Arthur River. If you are drawn here you will notice that The Edge of the World also has picnic tables, potable water and toilets, which are helpful when you are so far away from home.

64. EDIACARAN GOLD SPIKE

It's not gold and it's not even a spike. It's a bronze disc set in rock by the International Union of Geological Sciences to mark the world's official end of the Phanerozoic Eon (Cambrian Period) and the start of the Proterozoic Eon.

That's all meaningless to us mortals. What it really means is that the Ediacaran Period lasted from 635 million to 542 million years ago. This period is really important. It contains the first evidence of complex multicellular life on our planet. And, what is more, it was identified in 1946, in the Ediacara Hills of the Western Flinders Ranges by an Australian Geologist, Reg Sprigg. The fossil discovery site in the Ediacara Hills is closed to casual visitors and reserved for scientific research, but if you wish to view an actual Ediacaran fossil, buy an ice cream at the Beltana Roadhouse and ask to see their fossil; it's the one in the photo below.

The Ediacaran time period was formally adopted by the International Union of Geological Sciences in 2004 – the first new period added to the scale in 120 years. Furthermore, Ediacaran is the only name on the Geological Scale that originates from the Southern Hemisphere. The Ediacara Hills lie south-south-west of the Beltana Roadhouse and east of Lake Torrens.

The International Union of Geological Sciences is undertaking a new project to identify world reference points for the boundaries between geological time periods. Each point is marked by an inscribed bronze disc attached to the oldest rock layer of each time period. The Ediacaran Period Gold Spike is not located in the Ediacara Hills, but in a far more accessible location; an outcrop on the banks of a tributary of Brachina Creek (**#18**). But it's not marked or mentioned in the *Brachina Gorge Geological Trail* brochure. To find the gold spike turn north between information boards 1 and 2 along a short road signed 'Trezona Camp'. At the end of the road is a yellow sign instructing you to walk 400m along the trail to the gold spike. It's as easy as that! Once there walk down into the creek bed, look up, and it's on the creek bank. If you want to see the gold spike marking the end of the Ediacaran Period and the beginning of the next you will have to travel to Newfoundland, Canada.

65. ELLENBOROUGH FALLS

Ellenborough Falls are Australia's and the Southern Hemisphere's second-tallest waterfalls with a straight drop of 200m. (The tallest are Wallaman Falls (**#208**) west of Ingham in Queensland.) So, if you're close by, take a look. The roads from both Port Macquarie and Taree to the falls are part gravel,

Photo: Shutterstock | ArtInDigital

but normally suitable for passenger cars. You can drive to within 50m of the falls' top. The Bulga Plateau, from which the falls drop, was uplifted along with the Great Dividing Range 10 million years ago. Since then, the Ellenborough River and Falls have been cutting back along an older existing fault line. Evidence of the fault can be seen by looking down valley and noting its straightness. Rivers find it easy to erode along fault lines as the rocks along a fault have commonly been shattered by earth movements. The falls are now cutting back at right angles along an intersecting fault.

If when you visit you want further evidence for the fault, take a close look at the rocks on both sides of the valley. The rocks you can see in the river bed above the falls are soft sedimentaries (below) from less than 300 million years ago. If you take the track towards 'The Knoll' on the other side you will find much older and harder rocks. This Knoll side was caught up in the big squeeze that formed the Lachlan Fold Belt. The rocks over there are at least 550 million years old and formed in a deep ocean environment.

66. ELLERY CREEK BIG HOLE

Ellery Creek is the most important geological site in central Australia. Rocks to the north of the gap belong to the very ancient Arunta Block that is more than a billion years old, although you can't see these granites

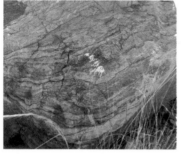

and metamorphic rocks at Ellery Creek as they are overlaid by the 850-million- to 800-million-year-old red quartzites that greet you on your arrival at the Big Hole. From 800 million to 760 million years ago shallow water covered the older quartzite allowing for the deposition of dolomite and siltstone. Between 760 million and 620 million years ago the region was near the North Pole as evidenced by the glacial material that fell from melting icebergs above onto the limestones

Contorted rocks at Ellery Big Hole.

and shales below. By around 340 million years ago the accumulated sandstone (pre-quartzite) and other sediments had reached a thickness estimated to be about 2km.

Then the unthinkable happened. Between 340 million and 300 million years ago continental Australia bumped into something that squeezed southern Australia against the north. The rocks of the Amadeus Basin buckled forming high mountains of the Himalayan type. I have seen it suggested that these mountains were at least 6,000m high. Over the following 300 million years these mountains have eroded to give us the MacDonnell and other east-west aligned ranges.

Ellery Big Hole is the start and finish of a 3km dolomite circuit that takes you past interesting rock structures and types. As the last mountain-building event left many strata standing almost on end, in just a kilometre or two you can view close to a billion years of geological history. All this and more, and it's free!

67. EMILY GAP

Like its sister, Jessie Gap, Emily has been formed by a tributary of the Todd River cutting north through a narrow section of the East MacDonnell Ranges. This was no easy task as the dominant rock strata here are quartzites. The strata stand at around 10° off vertical, tilted to this position more than 300 million years ago.

Emily Gap is a good place for a closer look at quartzite. Here the rock is polished clean by occasional floods. Try scratching it with another rock. The quartzite is shiny, smooth and very, very hard.

As you walk along the creek bed look closely at the base of the western wall. You will find this gaping crack (below left). It is an excellent example of how rocks may fracture when relieved of pressure that was once applied by the weight of other overlying rock.

Quartzite is metamorphosed sandstone. Under extreme heat and pressure the sandstone has partially melted and reverted to characteristics similar to its granitic origin. Like granite, quartzite also erodes to form sand.

68. EMMA FALLS

Photo: Yvonne Barrett.

Emma Falls are at the north-eastern end of the Kimberley Plateau. The plateau was gifted to us by an unknown large landmass that appears to have been anchored north of Australia around 2 billion years ago. (Indonesia did not exist at that time.) Large rivers flowing south on this landmass carried huge volumes of sand that spread over its nearby ocean floor. As the sediment increased in weight, the sea floor sank, making space available for the accumulation of more sediment. This sinking and sedimentation led to the formation of the Kimberley Basin.

Crustal movement caused weaknesses to develop in the Kimberley Basin allowing magma to break through. Lava flows increased the volume of material in the relatively young basin. In places, the combined depth of volcanic rock and sandstone exceed 5km.

After 200 million years this unrecognised landmass lifted anchor and drifted south and together with its Kimberley Basin crashed into northern Australia. The King Leopold and other ancient ranges running south-east from the Buccaneer Archipelago to Halls Creek and then north-east to near Kununurra were formed by this collision. The invading landmass then drifted away leaving the Kimberley Basin behind as if in some sort of reparation for having caused the accident and fleeing the scene. Such 'pin the tail on the donkey' add-ons to continents are referred to as terranes.

Crustal movements in the Kimberley east of Halls Creek around half a billion years ago formed the Mueller, O'Donnell and Carr Boyd Ranges. Around 200 million years ago a gentle uplift raised the basin floor above sea level. Another gentle uplift about 20 million years ago further raised the plateau creating sufficient slope for rivers to aggressively cut gorges back along fault and joint lines.

Water from Emma Gorge flows into the King River. Emma Gorge and Falls are on private land. Entry is via the El Questro Emma Gorge Resort. You must phone ahead.

Remnants of various ancient ranges between Halls Creek and Kununurra.

69. EUCLA SAND DUNES

The sand dunes at the old Eucla Telegraph Station are different to the dunes we normally find behind beaches. They're also different to the long parallel dunes found in the interior deserts.

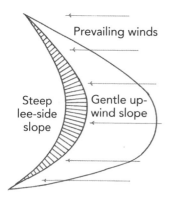

Prevailing winds

Steep lee-side slope

Gentle up-wind slope

Eucla's dunes are barchans – a jumble of coalescing crescent dunes that change their shape with changes in wind direction. Their short movements are backwards and forwards and around and about. They hover in this one area as if scared to break out and explore. Individual dunes have a gentle windward slope with sand grains bouncing up the slope until they fall over the back edge to form a steep, angle of rest. Barchans move downwind, but at Eucla the winds lose their strength as the air moves upward so as to clear the escarpment. As the barchans pile up on top of each other they lose their crescent shape and their long tails, but keep their steep back slopes.

The Eucla Dunes have formed in a small, protected part of the Great Australian Bight. To the east of the dunes is a solid rocky limestone

escarpment that rises above the surrounding plain. The dominant westerly winds are partially blocked by the escarpment and form swirling eddy currents as they rise over it. The relatively still air at the base of the ridge stops the sand's progress to the east while the dominant wind stops the sand spreading to the west. The sand grains are different too. They're not the usual sharp quartz crystals of granite or sandstone origin; these are Nullarbor limestone grains similar to those found on Kangaroo Island. You don't believe me? Put some in a glass or plastic container and add some vinegar. The mix will bubble and give off carbon dioxide gas as the acid dissolves the calcium carbonate. If that's too much of a bother, just pick up some and let it run through your fingers. This sand is light and soft.

70. FAN ROCK

Fan Rock, near Yeppoon, is just a small but spectacular part of a cluster of volcanic remnants in the area. The volcanoes erupted around 65 million to 75 million years ago. All the remnants are

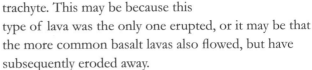

trachyte. This may be because this type of lava was the only one erupted, or it may be that the more common basalt lavas also flowed, but have subsequently eroded away.

Double Head, home of Fan Rock, formed as twin volcanic plugs covered by tens of metres of ash and fragmented rocks. Eruptions were sometimes explosive as gas and steam escaped into the atmosphere. Later eruptions pushed lava into the fractured mass, filling cracks and building dykes.

Fan Rock appears to have formed when lava was forced into and filled an existing narrow ravine. The top of this molten mass was most probably covered by hot ash erupted at the same time. The sides of the flow would have cooled by contact with the ravine sides while the bottom cooled by contact with the chasm's floor. As shrinkage cracks develop at right-angles to the cooling surfaces (**#33**), the cracks between the columns at Fan Rock indicate cooling from the base and from the sides. The ash and rubble from the top have since eroded away.

The fan is only a small section of the large solidified lava mass. Its eastern section has been massively eroded by the sea. The axis of the fan marks the original centre of the intrusion. The fan is only visible because the sea has eroded a cliffed gully to expose it. That same gully also separates viewers from the fan.

West of Fan Rock a group of trachyte remnants can be viewed from along the road from Yeppoon to Rockhampton. The one in the photograph (left) is a dome. Volcanic domes often form when viscous (thick, plasticine-like) lava is squeezed up under layers of ash.

71. FINGAL HEAD GIANT'S STAIRWAY

Mount Warning (opposite), where the morning sun first strikes the
Australian continent, is best recognised by its towering trachyte
plug and lava chamber. It was the largest of Australia's east coast
hot-spot volcanoes (**#49**). Mount Warning's footprint extended well into the
adjacent Pacific Ocean.

Unknown to many is the spectacular Giant's Causeway at Fingal Head a few
kilometres south of Tweed Heads. The name 'Giants Causeway' is obviously
derived from its namesake in Northern Ireland. Although this one is smaller, the
name is still appropriate. At Fingal Head, a 23-million-year-old Mount Warning
basalt lava flow has been exposed and washed clean by a rising Pacific Ocean. Sea
levels at the time of Mount Warning's eruptions were much lower than at present.
Cook Island, in the photograph (below), was also part of the same lava flow group.

The tightly packed, flat-sided columns developed when the original lava cooled
and contracted as it solidified (**#33**). The causeway is a peninsula from the mainland
and its neck is breached at high tide and by waves. Be warned! If you want a safe
close inspection of the columns, there are many more to be walked on and studied
where you stand to take photographs.

Mount Warning is 1,157m high. The plug section has a much smaller diameter than its bulbous lava chamber.

72. FINKE RIVER

Is the Finke River the oldest river in the world? Perhaps. Under most circumstances it is difficult to tell the age of a river, but with the Finke, it's different. In the photo (below) the Finke can be seen cutting across the West MacDonnell Ranges at Glen Helen in central Australia. These ranges formed under north-south compression between 350 million and 300 million years ago. If the river had formed after this time, surely it would have run east-west between the parallel ridges. The Finke is said to be antecedent; it existed prior to the mountain-building event and simply held its course by eroding its bed to match the rate of uplift.

Technically, the Finke commences where the Davenport and Ormiston Creeks merge, less than 1km upstream from Glen Helen Gorge. These two tributaries drain a vast area to the north of the West MacDonnell Ranges and they themselves are also antecedent. These two rivers and/or their branches have cut Simpsons Gap, Standley Chasm, Ellery Creek Big Hole, and Ormiston, Serpentine and Redbank Gorges.

The Finke's first gorge, Glen Helen (opposite above), just below the junction of the Davenport and Ormiston Creeks, is unlike the gorges upstream on the Finke's tributaries. Glen Helen is cut through sandstone, the others are in quartzite.

After cutting through the various ranges of the West MacDonnells the Finke cuts across the James Ranges that lie to the south. In doing so it has cut further gorges, one of which bears its name.

While confined within its gorge, the Finke runs mainly on a bed of solid rock and shallow rock pools, but between Hermannsburg and its gorge, the Finke is wide with a bed of sandy gravel. This part of the river is used as the only road to access Palm Valley, one of its tributaries. After overcoming the James Ranges the Finke turns south-east into South Australia heading for, but not making it to Lake Eyre.

73. FITZROY FALLS

Fitzroy Falls marks the point where Yarrunga Creek leaves
the tranquility of the Southern Tablelands to crash over the
escarpment on its way to join the Kangaroo River. The first drop
is a clear free-fall of 81m. After flowing below, in between and
around a number of house-sized boulders at the foot of the first fall, the creek
emerges to fall over a second rock-hugging section and then onward down its
forested valley. The two sections have a total height of 117m.

The sandstone at Fitzroy Falls was laid down under the sea commencing
some 250 million years ago along with the Blue Mountains' Sandstone and other
sandstones as far north as Gunnedah. A series of uplifts commencing around 70
million years ago lifted the sedimentary layers above sea level to eventually provide
the base for the Southern Tablelands. Erosion has removed some of the upper
strata, and lava flows have covered some of the area around Robertson.

Nature has been given a helping hand by the construction of a small reservoir
on Yarrunga Creek upstream from the falls. This ensures that visitors to the site,
even in times of drought, are almost guaranteed to see water flowing over the falls.
Other features provided by humans include well-made paths, a viewing platform
and an excellent visitor centre.

Photos: Shutterstock | crbellette (below) and (opposite) Shutterstock | Elias Bitar

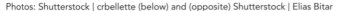

74. FLETCHER CROSSING

The Greenvale Highway crosses the world's longest lava flow at Fletcher Crossing, 40km north-west of Charters Towers. With a length of 120km, the Toomba Flow is not only the longest, but also among our youngest, and home to some of Australia's best-preserved volcanic landforms. Fletcher Crossing is of interest in that it illustrates the influence lava flows have on river drainage patterns and it's also a great example of lava-flow inflation.

This area was a gently sloping lava plain long before the Toomba Volcano erupted. The plain featured broad lava flows, through which rivers ran and cut their courses. Lolworth River was one of these. The Toomba Volcano erupted a large volume of very hot and very liquid basaltic lava around 13,000 years ago. The lava flowed downhill until it reached the Lolworth River, where upon it did the natural thing and flowed down the river's course boiling out its water as it went.

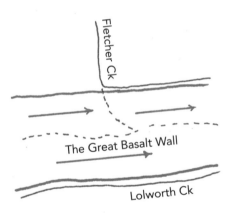

The snout of the lava flow did not stop until it reached the Burdekin River. Long parts of the flow inflated, forming what is now termed 'The Great Basalt Wall' (GBW). At Fletcher Crossing the highway crosses an uninflated section of the GBW.

Inflation is fascinating. How do you blow up (inflate) a lava flow? Lava flowing down a channel forms a crust. Turbulence in the flow usually breaks the crust into rafts that are carried along by the flow. If the rafts jam up, a continuous cover may form that insulates the still-flowing lava beneath. Any downstream slowing in flow (such as a narrowing of the channel) will cause the level of the flow behind the restriction to rise. Cracks in the crust fill with fresh lava that, on contact with the air, cools and reseals the flow's roof and growing sides. Repetition of this process can cause the flow to inflate by tens of metres. So that which starts as a river channel can become a long, sinuous, ridge. In the photo (opposite), the dry creek is Fletcher Creek. The ridge to the left of the creek is the GBW, an inflated flow formed in the bed of Lolworth Creek. The drainage patterns of Lolworth and Fletcher Creeks were rearranged by the Toomba Lava Flow. After the lava cooled, Lolworth Creek regained its water, but was forced to make a new course for itself on the southern side of the lava flow. Fletcher Creek, a minor northern tributary of the Lolworth, was blocked from entering the Lolworth and forced to flow down the other side of the lava to make a new junction with the Burdekin.

The Greenvale Highway crosses both creeks and an uninflated section of the GBW. Inflated sections of the lava flow can be viewed on the left just north of Fletcher Crossing, to the east by driving into the Dalrymple National Park and walking downstream, or by heading west along Red Falls Road to the Great Basalt Wall National Park.

The national park has been closed for several years due to dangerous conditions. Check at the Charters Towers Information Office.

75. FOSSIL BLUFF

Fossil Bluff is perched a couple of kilometres west of Wynyard on Tasmania's north coast. The cliff face is crammed full of marine fossils. The fossils are mainly of shells, snails and soft corals.

But you first need to put the fossils in context. Noticeboards at the site reveal that the rocks on the adjacent wave-cut platform are quite ancient. The oldest are 500-million-year-old sandstones and siltstones. On top of these are 300-million-year-old tillites; the droppings from icebergs and glaciers. Some granite boulders, originating hundreds of kilometres away from Fossil Bluff, are included in the droppings. This indicates that the glaciers must have been large.

At 1–2m above the platform there is an abrupt change from tillite to the fossil-bearing sandstone. The bottom of these strata is only 22 million years old. The top is covered by 13-million-year-old basalt from the close-by Table Mountain Volcano. The fossils are densest near the base of the sandstone, grading to sparse or non-existent just below the basalt. Please do not take samples as souvenirs.

76. FLYNNS BEACH SERPENTINITE

Port Macquarie beaches and headlands (bottom) are honeypots for lovers of interesting rocks. This thin 4km stretch of sand and rock is an accretionary complex. Never heard of one? These are

chunks of rock that continents occasionally pick up. The one at Port Macquarie was tacked onto south-east Australia by the spreading ocean floor of the Proto-Pacific Ocean around 400 million years ago. (At that time, New Zealand was nowhere near where it is now.) As the heavy ocean floor slid under a lightweight Australia, the lighter sediments were pushed down, metamorphosed (changed by heat and pressure), uplifted and then welded to the coast.

The Port Macquarie Accretion contains some very interesting, and in some cases, rare rocks. One of these rarities is serpentinite, which can be viewed at the southern end of Flynns Beach. The rock has a strong greenish tinge and is smooth and greasy to touch.

The serpentinite (top left) was originally upper mantle rock that came in contact with the ocean-floor basalt and seawater during the subduction. The contact, heat and pressure induced changes in the chemistry of the mantle rock. Under pressure, some of this modified mantle rock was squeezed to the surface as serpentinite. The dark blobs in the rock face are solid serpentinite; the paler-coloured sections are the same rock, but have experienced shearing, where rock fragments have slid across other fragments in the same manner that new playing cards slide on top of one another.

Other special rocks at Port Macquarie include blue schist at Rocky Beach (above centre), pillow lava and chert. A very informative guide to the rocks is available at the Tourist Info Centre.

77. FRASER ISLAND LAKES

Fraser Island is home to the world's largest collection of perched lakes. On the island are 20 larger and a number of smaller perched lakes; Lake McKenzie (opposite below) is a fine example. Perched freshwater lakes sit high in the sand dunes with their bottoms well above sea level. They have developed in sand depressions over thousands of years. The lakes form when leaves accumulate in a depression inducing it to hold water for short periods following rain. The leaves eventually decay to form humus. Fine sand and dust gets caught in the water, sinks to the bottom and further clog the bed. In this manner the lakebed increases in size, thickness and water-holding capacity. Any vegetation which was in the lake dies and adds to the humus. The lake water is exceptionally

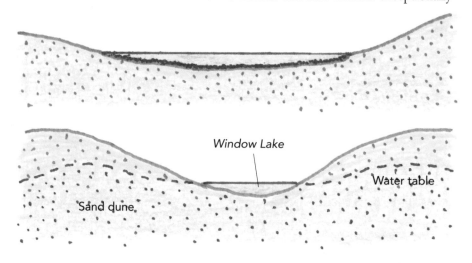

pure but has a low pH level due to the release of humic acid, a by-product of rotting vegetation. To humans the strength of acid is weak and its dilution renders it completely harmless. The water is exceptionally clear and soft.

Perched lakes are not the only type of lake to be found on Fraser Island. Wabby Lake is termed a barrage lake as it formed by the blocking of a spring-fed stream by a sand blow.

Yankee Jack and Ocean Lakes are window lakes. Window lakes form when the water table rises above the bottom of a depression in the sand. It should be noted that the water table – the line that separates the zone of saturation from the zone above which contains some air – is not horizontal, but tends to follow the general shape of the surface.

78. FRENCHMAN PEAK

Frenchman Peak was named for its shape, which supposedly looks like a 19th-century Frenchman's cap. Although not stirring my imagination, the peak is really interesting. It illustrates an important element of granite's general shape. Granite (**#55**) features tend to be rounded. Look at the photos; everything is rounded, almost smooth. Large slabs have split from the dome and are poised ready to slide down to the bottom of the slope. And slide they will when it's wet and slippery enough for gravity to win over inertia. The large pile of broken rock at the foot of the slope (not visible in the photographs) is ample evidence that these slips do occur. The cap sitting on top of the dome would slip except it's too flat up there. Even the smaller slab forming the peak appears poised to slide into oblivion. All this granite solidified under tremendous pressure more than a billion years ago.

Up close, Frenchman Peak is remarkable in that a tunnel passes right through the cap and there are other small cave-like indentations in its surface. These features are formed by cavernous weathering and are termed tafoni. Cavernous weathering is caused by the combined presence of salt and moisture. Dissolved salt can penetrate the minute cracks that separate granite's crystals one from another. The salt solution is sea spray, blown in by wind. As the surface dries the water evaporates and the salt precipitates forcing the crystals apart. Repetition of this process gradually removes particles of rock one at a time eventually forming caves. Granites (and some sandstones) often develop an impervious coating, commonly called 'desert varnish' that protects the surface. Cavernous weathering establishes itself on fresh surfaces before desert varnish can form.

But is the tunnel tafoni? There's a possibility that the tunnel was originally cut by ocean waves. Around 40 million years ago sea levels were at least 300m above current levels, which would mean that only the top of Frenchman Peak was above water around that time. Most of the other Cape Le Grand peaks were submerged. This possibility is supported by evidence of wave-cut platforms near the peak. The tunnel may or may not have resulted from wave action, but cavernous weathering is certainly working there now.

79. GARDENS OF STONE

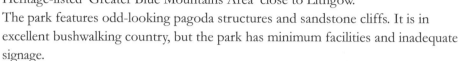

This relatively new national park (1994) is part of the World
Heritage-listed 'Greater Blue Mountains Area' close to Lithgow.
The park features odd-looking pagoda structures and sandstone cliffs. It is in
excellent bushwalking country, but the park has minimum facilities and inadequate
signage.

The crucial part of a pagoda lies in its ironstone capping. The pagodas lie
close to, but separate from, the cliffed escarpments. Most of Australia's sandstone
contains some iron, but the content in the pagodas is far more than normal. The
sandstone in this area near Cullen Bullen was overlaid by basalt lava flows less than
20 million years ago. All that basalt has weathered and eroded away. During the
process of weathering the iron, a common ingredient of basalt, was dissolved and
carried down into the underlying sandstone. The presence of clay in some strata
stopped this downward movement. The iron precipitated at this level, forming a
harder and more resistant layer.

Once the ironstone capping has been removed by further erosion, the pagoda
formations assume more of a bee-hive shape.

80. GEIKIE GORGE

Towards the end of the Devonian Period, from 416 million to 358 million years ago, coral reefs formed in the shallow seas that then almost encircled the Kimberley. Portions of those ancient reefs, including Geikie Gorge, still exist and are protected in a number of national parks and conservation reserves. On the surface, these long thin strips of limestone resemble low, sharp, pygmy mountain ranges. But in reality, they are a 'last man standing' type of landform, the remains left after all else has eroded away.

The reefs are unlike present reefs in that they were built mainly from algae and other lime-excreting organisms more so than coral. The reefs consisted of numerous isolated atolls and long barrier chains, some more than 100km long. During the reefs' growing years the sea floor gradually sank, but the reef-building organisms grew at the same rate, building limestone that in places reached an incredible 2km in thickness. About 100 million years later the sea floor rose exposing the reefs to the surface. This was followed by a further period of subsidence when the reefs fell below sea level and became covered by sandstones and mudstones. About 20 million years ago the area was again uplifted and became subject to erosion. All the young sandstones and mudstones have eroded away. As limestone weathers and erodes more slowly than most other sedimentary rocks, the limestone ranges now stand 40–150m above the surrounding plain.

Geikie Gorge has been cut by Australia's largest river when measured by flood flow; the Fitzroy. The annual summer flood raises the water height in the gorge by 12–20m. This flooding cleans the rock that lies below flood level and exposes the strata in their true colours which are shades of white. The cliffs above the flood are either grey with lichen, or orange where sections have recently fallen into the river. The orange splashes are from oxidising iron. The upper surface of the reef is rough and difficult to cross.

81. THE GEMFIELDS

Just short of 50km west of Emerald lie three small villages: Anakie, Sapphire and Rubyvale. Collectively these three are known as 'The Gemfields' and they are a major source of Australian sapphires and rubies. Both gemstones are closely related as they are forms of corundum, a natural compound of aluminium and oxygen (Al_2O_3). Blue is the traditional colour of sapphires, but they can also be found as yellow, green, purple, peach or clear stones. Red and pink colouring leads to stones being classified as rubies. Colour comes from impurities in the corundum. The presence of pure chromium gives rubies their red-pink colour, while various combinations of iron, titanium and chromium are responsible for the colour in sapphires.

Sapphires and rubies have a geological history similar to that of diamonds (**#4**). They are formed under extreme pressure in the mantle beneath the Earth's crust. They are brought to the surface by volcanic eruptions and lie trapped in volcanic rock until the rock erodes. The gems are then washed into streams where they become buried in sand and gravel. Normally they do not travel far from their origin due to their high weight-to-size ratio. Sapphires are second only to diamonds in hardness among natural minerals.

If you are a fossicker you head for the creek with hat, shovel, other equipment, a strong back and a keen eye, but make sure you're in a public fossicking area and not on someone else's private claim.

If you are a fair dinkum miner, you dig a hole down to the granite bedrock. Once there you hope to find a layer of gravel lying on top of the granite which in turn is covered by a weakly cemented layer of sandstone. The three layers, fine sandstone at the top, then weak gravel conglomerate sitting on solid granite, can be clearly seen in the photograph (right above).

And when you find it, a rough sapphire is just a dark pebble with the flat sides of a crystal.

82. GIRRAWEEN PYRAMID

New England is home to one of eastern Australia's largest bodies of granite. It stretches 400km from Stanthorpe, Queensland, to the Moonbi Ranges south of Tamworth, New South Wales, and is certainly large enough to be classified as a batholith. Just to jog your memory of high school Ancient Greek, batholith means 'deep rock'. And deep it is. It goes all the way

down to the bottom of the Earth's crust. This granite mass formed at this location, or floated up to it, around 240 million years ago. Most of the thousands of metres of sedimentary rock, part of the Tasman Fold Belt (**#116**) that lay above the granite, has eroded away. It is thought that the granite was exposed within 50 million years of its formation. So what you see now is the result of 190 million years of weathering and erosion. A border-straddling cluster of three national parks – Girraween, Boonoo Boonoo and Bald Rock – are granite wonderlands.

The dominant peak in Girraween is its 'Pyramid'. It can be climbed by the fit and adventurous. The eye-catching line of squarish blocks that slash diagonally across the face of the dome is not a fault line, just a great example of granite disintegrating along surface-paralleling and perpendicular joint lines. As pressure was reduced by the removal of overburden, the granite cracked and expanded (**#55**).

The loose blocks have separated from the top layer of granite along a surface-paralleling joint and slid down the face of the layer beneath. The sliding was made possible by the steepness of the slope and an abundant supply of water. During cold periods of the last ice age the mountain would have experienced frosts and probably snow. These blocks will eventually weather, become rounded and slide and/or roll to the bottom of the slope.

83. GLASS HOUSE MOUNTAINS

The Glass House Mountains are a part of a short eastern hot-spot chain of volcanoes stretching south from Indian Head at the northern end of Fraser Island. The Glass Houses were active volcanoes between 27 million and 25 million years ago. Geologically, all 13 peaks are the one volcano and sourced from the one subterranean molten reservoir. At

Glass House Mountains from Mary Cairncross Scenic Reserve.

the time of the eruptions, lava rising to the surface comprised mainly trachyte and/or rhyolite rather than the much more common basalt.

Trachyte and rhyolite lavas both tend to be very thick, much like ultra-hot plasticine. On reaching the surface they do not flow very far before solidifying and blocking their vents. When the volcano next erupts it finds its former vent blocked and is forced to find a new exit to the surface. The 13 Glass Houses mark 13 different eruptions from the one reservoir of magma. When the volcano was active the peaks would have been covered by ash and other loose material. That material has since eroded away.

Below left: Mount Coonowrin (Crooked Neck). Below right: The Twins. Bottom: Mount Tibrogargan.

84. COASTAL SAND MOVEMENT

Regular beachgoers are familiar with changes in shape to their favourite stretch of sand. Yes it's caused by waves, but how and why?

Constant winds blowing across water cause waves to form. The wider the stretch of water, the more regular the waves. Gentle winds form constructive waves (opposite top) that break forwards and stir up small amounts of sand. The sand is carried forward and up the beach by the swash. Most of the swash sinks back into the beach and the moved sand is deposited.

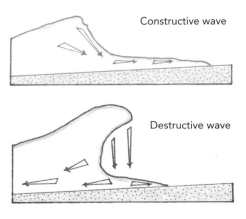

Constructive wave

Destructive wave

Stronger storm winds build larger waves that may form a different shape. Crests of these waves overhang the wave body and break vertically, stirring up a large volume of sand. Most of the breaking water returns directly back into the ocean and carries with it the sand that it has stirred up. Such waves are destructive and tear away at the beach. It may take weeks of constructive waves to undo the damage of a day or two of destructive waves.

More important than its in-and-out movement is sand's lateral movement. Such movement can be caused by waves breaking at an angle to the beach, causing beach drifting, or within the surf, which is termed longshore drifting.

Beach drifting takes place on the damp part of the beach. It consists of the swash, where broken waves run up the beach until their forward motion stops, and then the backwash takes over, where the water runs back to the sea.

If the waves strike a beach at an angle, sand grains are carried up the beach at the same angle, but they return perpendicular to the coast effectively moving the sand laterally.

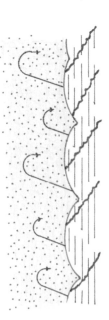

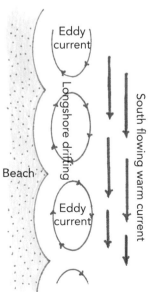

Eddy
current

Longshore drifting

South flowing warm current

Beach

Eddy
current

Longshore drifting is driven by ocean currents and takes place in the surf, where waves break. Although examples are found all around the Australian Coast, the best are along the east coast, from south-east Tasmania to Townsville, Queensland. Here the main ocean current flows from north to south bringing warm water to the southern beaches. However, the near shore currents are eddies from the main current, and near the beach flow from south to north. As waves break, for a short period of time, sand is lifted off the ocean floor and becomes suspended. While suspended, the current carries these grains some millimetres northward before they fall again to the ocean floor. Each movement is miniscule, but occurs five or six times a minute, 24 hours a day, 365 days a year and has been doing so for at least the last 50 million years.

85. GOLD COAST SAND

By far and away Queensland's greatest import by volume from
New South Wales is sand: billions and billions of tonnes of
it. This movement of goods requires no human effort, costs
nothing and has been going on for millions of years. And what
does Queensland do with this sand? It builds islands and beaches so efficiently
that the state not only owns the world's largest sand island, but also its second and
its third (Fraser Island: 1,840km^2; North Stradbroke: 275km^2; Moreton:186 km^2).
Stories regarding the beaches along the Gold Coast, Moreton Bay, Sunshine Coast,
around Noosa and on to Fraser Island dominate the world's travel magazines.

Surfers Paradise beach.

Most of the sand originates from New England's granite and is transported to the coast via the Richmond and Clarence Rivers. Once the sand reaches the ocean it is moved north by two processes – longshore drifting and beach drifting (**#84**).

The Moreton Bay islands and Gold Coast beaches are intermediate stopovers in the building of Fraser Island 200km or so to the north. The beaches and islands are in a continuous state of change as sand is moved from one place to another. According to Wikipedia the Stradie Islands were joined until the late 1890s when a fierce storm forced a passageway through from the ocean to the Gold Coast Broadwater at Jumpinpin. Danger to boats and shipping's using of the new passage forced governments to construct the Gold Coast Seaway just to the north of Southport.

Dredging, sand pumping and the construction of new islands to deflect sand movement to the east of the seaway have, so far, appeared to have been effective in keeping the seaway open. One can confidently predict that eventually this whole coast will be straightened; Moreton and Deception Bays will be filled in or become brackish lakes.

86. GOSSE BLUFF

Like a walled medieval city without a city, Gosse Bluff sits on the
Amadeus Plain just west of the MacDonnell Ranges. It is one of a
small number of excellent Australian sites which are the result of
impacts by extraterrestrial bodies. Comets, meteors and meteorites
have been smashing into Australia ever since the continent was first forming.
In the earliest part of the Earth's geological history the surface must have looked
much like that of the moon today. As the Solar System matured most of these
heavenly objects were eliminated as they crashed into the planets or the sun. But
there are still billions of them out there. Large ones, when they crash into Earth,
release huge quantities of energy, blasting immense craters, pulverising rock and
throwing enormous quantities of dust into the atmosphere. The formation visible
at Gosse Bluff is a small section of the original crater's base.

About 140 million years ago a meteor travelling at an estimated speed of
2,500km per minute crashed into the surface of the Earth, blasting a crater
more than 2km deep and more than 20km wide. The force was so great that the
sedimentary rocks at the base of the crater beneath the point of impact were
shattered and depressed and those near the sides were pushed up. It is the pushed
up sides and shattered base that are now exposed. Two vertical kilometres of rocky
debris that previously lay above the present surface have been removed by erosion.
The crater remnant is 4.5km wide.

Top and centre: Inside the crater. Above: The road into Gosse Bluff is signposted off Namatjira Drive.

87. GREAT BARRIER REEF

A coral reef is nature's version of living rock. It is limestone in the making. Off the coast of Queensland lies the world's largest coral reef, 2,300km long and up to 75km wide. Actually, it's not a single reef, but a mass of around 3,000 reefs and nearly 1,000 islands. It is the world's largest structure made by living organisms. And that living organism is a very small animal, the coral polyp.

There have been coral reefs of one sort or another along this part of the continent's edge for around 500,000 years, but the reef in its current position is only about 8,000 years old. At the height of the last ice age, around 60,000–12,000 years ago, oceans were cooler and sea levels were around 130m below those of today. As a result, Australia's Pacific coast was much further east; in some places by around 100km. Warming commenced around 15,000 years ago and temperatures rose for the next 8,000 years to a point probably about 1°C above those experienced today. Ocean temperatures and sea levels rose accordingly and an environment suitable for coral growth developed. The growing part of the coral reef moved west towards the land as

the water levels rose. At the same time, some on the eastern edge coral died as the deepening water blocked sunlight from reaching the ocean floor. With a warming of the ocean, coral reefs also spread southwards to eventually colonise most of the area as we now know it.

There are four common types of reefs found along the Great Barrier Reef: fringing, platform, ribbon and cay. Fringing reefs, as found around

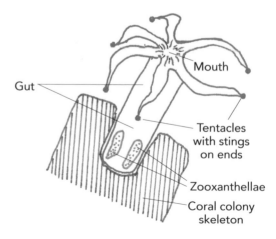

Photo: Shutterstock | Timothy Baxter

Magnetic Island, are the simplest form; they encircle the continental islands close to the mainland coast. Platform reefs lie in the sheltered waters between the outer reefs and the mainland. They are usually circular to oval in shape and range in size from several hectares to hundreds of hectares in size. Cays are small platform reefs that have accumulated sand along their edges. Well known cays include Lowe, Green, Heron, Lady Elliott and Lady Musgrave (**#117**) Islands.

Reefs are built by billions upon billions of coral polyps. These polyps are actually live individual animals varying in size from 3–50mm in both diameter and height. Hard corals have a calcium carbonate (limestone) cup-shaped base that is anchored to either a rock or more commonly, to a dead polyp. The calcium carbonate is extracted by the polyps from seawater.

88. GREAT ARTESIAN BASIN

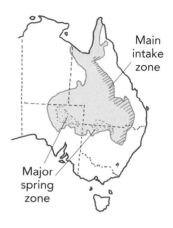

Main intake zone

Major spring zone

Everyone is aware of the importance of the Great Artesian Basin to Australia's economic wellbeing. Most know that the Basin is large. Some also know that it is the largest artesian basin in the world. It is estimated to contain 64 million million litres of water – a volume that is difficult or impossible to comprehend, but put another way the Great Artesian Basin holds about 130,000 times the capacity of Sydney Harbour.

The basin's water is held trapped between layers of impervious rocks that have a high clay content. The layer that holds the water is poorly consolidated sand and sandstone. Water-bearing layers are referred to as aquifers.

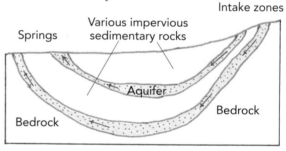

Back around 250 million years ago the basin area was reasonably flat and above sea level. Earth movements after that time caused the western and eastern sides of the basin to rise. Large rivers (it was not a desert at that time) eroded the highlands, washing in huge quantities of sand and mixed silt, mud and clay. The sand became the aquifers; the silt, mud and clay, the covering strata. As the sediment accumulated the basin sank under its own weight. The deepest sediments are now 3,000m below the surface. If you think about it, you could bury Mount Kosciuszko in there and nothing would show.

Fortunately, the main intake zones are reasonably well watered and some are covered by basalt lava flows. The basalt assists by allowing water to move quickly down from the surface. In the photo (opposite centre), water can be seen flowing over the tops of basalt columns exposed in the bed of a river. Water percolates down through the gaps between columns to start on its long trek to outlet springs to the south-west. Once in the aquifers, water moves at 1–5m per year. Water at some outlet springs in South Australia (opposite below and **#207**) is almost 2 million years old. Coarse sandstone rock along the eastern edge of the basin also plays a major role in topping up the basin's water level.

Above: Basin windmill pump and storage. Below: Water flowing over tops of basalt columns.

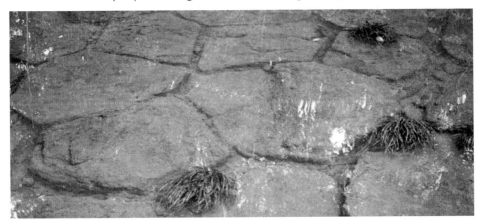

Above: South Australian Basin outlet spring.

Page 142

89. GREENFIELD SILICON BEACH

Jervis Bay travel promotions claim that the beach sand within the bay is the whitest in Australia. The sand is certainly different; it's soft to touch, not gritty between the toes and bright white. Scientists give some credence to the claim by informing us that the sand contains a higher percentage of silicon and less of silica than is found on most beaches.

Greenfield Beach.

Silicon is an element (Si), while silica is a compound of silicon and oxygen (SiO_2). Silica is found in large quantities as quartz in rocks such as granite and sandstone. Nearly all beach sand in Australia and the rest of the world is dominated by silica. Silicon sand is somewhat rare. Over time the Jervis Bay sand has had its unstable and some dissolvable minerals removed primarily by acid.

Prior to the last ice ages the bay was a river valley lying within a local syncline (downfold). Evidence for this can be seen in the dipping rocks behind Greenfield Beach and those on the eastern side of Beecroft Peninsula. At the end of the age, around 15,000 years ago, the slowly rising sea gradually filled the valley. Decaying vegetation increased the acidity of water that entered the almost enclosed bay. The few remaining small non-perennial creeks that enter the bay carry insufficient silt and vegetative debris to discolour the water and the sand, but still add acid to the poorly flushed bay waters.

90. HALLETT COVE

Commencing about 280 million years ago, Australia, as part of Gondwana, experienced an ice age that lasted for about 10 million years. Ice, several kilometres thick, covered two thirds of the continent. Scratches on bedrock at Hallett Cove are clearly visible in the nature reserve (bottom right, above).

When the glacier melted a large lake formed at Hallett Cove and millions of tonnes of sand and clay were deposited on top of the bedrock which had formed the lake bed. Such deposits are termed moraine. A recently eroded section of moraine, the 'Sugarloaf' (centre of top photo), forms the reserve's focal point.

The main body of the Sugarloaf is white sand. At its base is a layer of clay and boulders dropped by the glacier as it melted. The brown layer of clay at the top of the Sugarloaf has nothing to do with the glacier. The clay is of quite recent origin, having been deposited by a stream that ran through this area between 1 million and 2 million years ago.

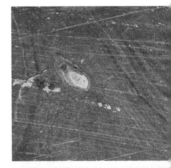

Away from the deeply eroded Sugarloaf region of the reserve are a number of large erratics. Erratics are boulders that have fallen onto the top of a glacier as it moves along scouring out the sides of mountains. These erratics (right) are carried along on the surface of the ice and deposited when the glacier finally melts. They are termed erratics because they are commonly of a different rock type to the rock on which they are found lying.

91. HAMELIN POOL SHELL-BLOCK

Shell-block is a halfway stage in limestone formation between being loose shells on a beach to becoming solid rock. Over the last few million years, seashells have been accumulating in this part of Hamelin Bay. They have built a layer that is now many metres deep. Pounding waves have smashed many to form a weak natural cement that holds the remaining shells and shell fragments together. In the past, shell-block was cut using crosscut-saws and used in the construction of buildings. It is soft,

From this ...

... to this.

lightweight, easily cut and has excellent insulation qualities. Areas that have been mined can be recognised by the rows of terraces cut into the shell fields. When used for construction, the shell block (left) looks very much like common concrete block. Mining of shell-block is now forbidden except to repair existing shell-block buildings and chainsaws are now used in the cutting.

The shell-block beach is found on the landward side of the famous stromatolites in the Shark Bay Marine Park (**#183**). The beach is made entirely from small cockleshells brought to the area by waves and ocean currents. The mined area lies between the beach and the Telegraph Station Museum.

The natural disintegration of this discarded block (above) at the quarry indicates just how weakly cemented some top layer blocks are; however, lower blocks are of better quality.

Shell block was used in the construction of the church and other buildings in Denham and the local area.

92. HANGING ROCK (MOUNT DIOGENES)

Hanging Rock is best known as the setting for the children's story and film *Picnic at Hanging Rock*. But for nature lovers, it's the location for one of the many east Australian hot-spot chains' last hurrah.

Mount Diogenes (below) and nearby Camels Hump (opposite above) are the 6-million-year-old remnants of eruptions that brought to an end the above ground huffing and puffing of a string of volcanoes stretching from south-east Queensland to Mount Diogenes and Camels Hump in Victoria. Both remnants are trachyte plugs. The pair are unusual examples of volcanoes sitting on top of another volcano. They sit on the sides of Mount Macedon, an extinct volcano. But the family connection is between Diogenes and Camels Hump and not with Mount Macedon. Mount Macedon last erupted nearly 400 million years ago and the fact that all share the same location is one of chance rather than them being caused by any particular weakness in the Earth's crust at that site.

When the viscous (thick and tacky) trachyte of Diogenes' lava cooled, it formed huge columns up to 5m in diameter, similar to those found in basalt (**#33**). These columns have weathered and eroded to form the mazes at the top of Mount Diogenes (opposite centre).

STEP-BY-STEP DEVELOPMENT OF MOUNT DIOGENES

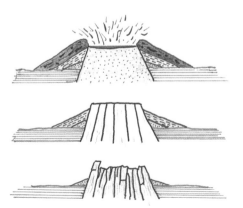

Stage 1 Trachyte eruption with fountaining and build-up of loose spatter, scoria and ash around the vent.

Stage 2 Eruption ceases and trachyte cools forming thousands of huge columns. Erosion quickly removes the loose material.

Stage 3 Erosion continues. Water penetrates cracks between the columns and permits erosion to enlarge these cracks and form maze.

93. HARMAN VALLEY LAVA BLISTERS

Some of the world's best examples of tumuli can be found near
the town of Byaduk along Old Crusher Road. The tumuli are
well signposted from the road into the Mount Eccles National Park and from
Byaduk. There are only two other places where such tumuli are found: Iceland and
Africa. The tumuli are circular with diameters of 10–20m and heights of 2–4m.

There are more than 30 tumuli
in the area with some less than
100m apart.

The tumuli were formed
when a lava flow from Mount
Napier (left) spread over a
swamp and small stream. The
generated steam was neither
explosive nor in huge volumes
as the heating of the water was
from the top down rather than
from the bottom up, and the
water was not held under great
compression. The resulting
steam applied pressure to the
underneath of the stationary
molten, but crusted, lava.
The pressure was sufficiently
great for some weak points
in the crust to break and
dome upwards to relieve the pressure. As the lava domed and cracked fresh lava
partially filled and sealed the cracks allowing the dome to be forced even higher.

It is thought that the
process of forming
blisters was relatively
fast – estimated to have
taken from only 12
hours to several days to
complete.

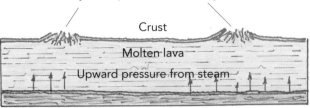

Weak points in crust dome upwards to release pressure
created by swamp water converting into steam

Crust

Molten lava

Upward pressure from steam

94. HARTZ MOUNTAINS ROCHE MUTONNEES

Roche Mutonnee is a French term and easily translates for non-Francophones as 'rock-mountain', which is totally wrong. 'Roche' is rock, but 'mouton' is sheep, so it's simply a sheep-like rock. So what do you call a half-dozen of them? A mob? Or perhaps a flock?

If you do the easy Hartz Mountain National Park Lake Osborne Walk from the car park towards Lake Osborne you will pass a group of superb roche mutonnees. As walkers crests the track after its gentle upward slope, rocky shapes come into their view on their left. These rocky pimples were constructed under a small icefield that straddled the high country from Hartz Mountain to Taylors Ridge.

The icefield flowed from the south (left side in all photos) to the north (right side). How do we know this? Because roche moutonnees have steeper slopes facing the direction from which the ice came and gentler slopes facing down the route the glacier was heading. The rock here is sandstone. The moving ice was more than 100m thick and scoured off the surface. As the ground surface was lowered, a number of more resistant patches of hard sandstone were encountered

beneath the ice. The glacier, acting like a thick liquid, simply over-rode and flowed around these obstacles to continue on its way. But, as the glacier passed over the obstacle, the rocks carried at the bottom of the glacier snagged at the upper surface of the obstacle, smoothing it off and producing a gentler back slope.

95. HASTINGS HOT SPRINGS

Some come here just to swim, others are here for the caves; it's a pity, but many of these visitors don't even look for the natural springs.

Way back when, around 600 million years ago, there were no caves or springs around here – just a layer of dolerite forming on a shallow seabed. And 'here' wasn't here – it was about 10° north of the Equator.

The hot springs at Hastings (bottom right) have little to do with the Hastings Caves (bottom left) that are 5km further up the road. Water at the springs originates from higher up above the caves and slowly percolates down through the ancient rocks and dolerite until it reaches a major fault 600–700m below the surface. Rock temperatures increase at about 25°C per kilometre as you go towards the centre of the Earth. Such a rate suggests that the water would reach temperatures of around 40°C. Pressure from the water above moving down forces the warm water to rise to the surface along the fault line. It reaches the surface at temperature of between 27–29°C.

The springs can be viewed from a well-made track that starts near the swimming pool. The springs are difficult to photograph due to the mottled light and bubbling water. But they're well worth the short flat walk and the little effort necessary for you to view them.

Hastings Caves are in dolomite; limestone with an added dash of magnesium. Dolerite is harder than limestone, but is equally dissolved by weak acid.

96. HENBURY METEORITE CRATERS

The Henbury Meteorite Craters are fairly normal as far as
meteorite craters go. What's abnormal though, is that such craters
are accessible; just 12km west of Australia's only central north-
south highway; the Stuart. This cluster of craters formed between 4,000 and 5,000
years ago, so they're almost new. The largish iron-nickel meteorite disintegrated
just prior to impact, splitting into four significant pieces, eight smaller ones and

numerous even smaller fragments. The largest pieces are estimated to have been
around the size of a 200-litre (44-gallon) drum with each weighing more than a
tonne. Thousands of small fragments have been scavenged from the site and few
remain. The largest recovered piece, over 40kg in weight, is exhibited in the Alice
Springs Museum.

Two of the larger portions fell close together, forming coalescing craters that
have depths of 15m and a combined width of 180m. A dark peninsula jutting out
from the north-eastern rim marks the division between the two craters (below
right). A third crater is separated from the combined two by a distinct debris wall.

The fourth major crater, the Water Crater (below left), lies adjacent to the
others, forming a triangle. Its name 'Water' follows from its southern wall having
been breached by a small seasonal creek. Its flat floor partially fills with water and
becomes boggy following rain (which is not often). The floor is covered by grass
and ringed by trees.

97. HENTY GLACIAL MORAINE

The Henty Moraine is marked on many maps. It's at the side of
the A10 Highway north-west of Queenstown, just a couple of
hundred metres short of its junction with the B28 to Tullah. A moraine is a pile
of rocky material deposited by a glacier as it melts. The Henty Moraine contains
a number of large erratics; rocks that have been transported from their original
position by a glacier. The erratics at the Henty Moraine were moved more than
20km from north of Mount Julia. The glacier in the Henty River Valley was large
by Australian standards – 20km long, at least 2km wide and more than 200m thick.

A large erratic sits at the side of the car park (below left). Others sit along a
well-trodden track leading from the edge of the road up along the moraine and
past some huge truck-sized erratics to reach a memorial to a prominent geologist.
The most amazing of the erratics – the first you encounter along the track – bears
striations (scratches) along one side. Most striations are caused by rocks imbedded
in a glacier scraping over the bedrock. The one in the photograph (below right)
is much more than a single scratch; it's a massive groove at least a metre wide and
nearly half a metre deep. It was made in a similar manner to a simple striation, but
was made by hundreds of thousands of scratches all following the same direction
and channelled along the same line. This piece of once-solid rock has been plucked
from the valley floor, transported, and then dumped at an angle of 90° to its
original orientation.

Further along the track is a pair of a fortuitously placed balancing erratics
(opposite). Both rocks have been carried along on the same glacier. As the glacier
melted, the smaller particles of morainal material were washed away gradually
lowering the smaller erratic to come to rest on top of a larger erratic.

98. HIDDEN VALLEY (MIRIMA)

Hidden Valley, the name by which Mirima National Park is most
commonly known, is a small piece of dry land at the southern
end of the Bonaparte Basin. The Bonaparte Basin forms the floor
of the Timor Sea into which the Ord River flows. Hidden Valley
has a wide diversity of landform shapes on display, varying from miniature Kings
Canyon (**#114**) style red cliffs, to sections that appear to have been bitten out by
giant rock-eating dinosaurs.

The condensed geological history of the area goes like this. Around 400 million
to 500 million years ago sediment began filling a geologic basin that lies to the
north of Australia. However, the rocks in Mirima are much younger than that.
They're only about a quarter that age as they lie on top of the original deposits.
The edge of the basin was forced against Australia some 70 million years ago,
causing this part of the basin to be raised above sea level. Since then, erosion by
the Ord River and its tributaries has cut steep valleys into the soft sandstone.

The algae that cover the exposed rock at Mirima lead to comparisons being
made between it and the Bungles (**#173**). This is both misleading and unfair.
The algae is in blotches, while the parallel lines at Mirima (below left) are from
variations in average grain sizes from one stratum to the next. Sand grains
laid down in strong currents are coarser than grains deposited under calmer
conditions. When these grains were cemented into rock, these slight differences
become accentuated with different strata weathering and eroding at different rates.
'Differential weathering' is used as the term to describe such features. This 'stack
of pancakes' style landform is common in sandstone worldwide.

Mirima boasts fine examples of cross-bedding (opposite page, right) in its strata. These easily spotted non-conforming strata are exposed on cliff sides. Cross-bedding occurred here when a fast-flowing stream formed sandbars across its mouth where it entered the sea. The parallel but inclined strata mark the advancing leading edge of the bar. Changes in current can lead to an abrupt change in its shape.

99. HORIZONTAL FALLS

The Kimberley Coast contains some of the most dramatic scenery in the world. It's a pity that it's so remote and so poorly serviced by roads. On the other hand, this is one of its beauties. The surreal feeling it generates for visitors leaving their cares and the pressures of the world behind is part of its attraction.

One of the Kimberley's most intriguing attractions is Horizontal Falls, located in Talbot Bay at the northern end of the Buccaneer Peninsula.

Two small sections of the bay are separated from the main body of water by narrow gaps running through two ridges of the McLarty Ranges. The northern gap (opposite, foreground) is approximately 20m wide while the southern one is only 10m wide. The distance between the two gaps is approximately 300m. As the flows through the gaps cannot keep pace with the rising tide, water banks up against both gaps. Landward-flowing waterfalls are created with a rising tide. When high tide is reached, equilibrium exists for a very short period of time until the outgoing tide causes the water to flow back through the gaps to the ocean. The outflow is most spectacular as the flow is forced through the narrower of the two gaps first. The height differential between water levels in the smaller inlet and Talbot Bay can be as great as 4m (below).

The tidal range on this section of coast can be up to 10m. The mega-tides are caused by the funnel shape of many of the bays along the coast and by the gentle incline of the ocean floor towards the land.

Interest has been expressed by some for the damming of one or two bays along the Kimberley Coast to utilise the reversing waterfall effect to produce hydro-electricity for Darwin.

Photo: Carol Moore.

Photo: Stewart Barrett.

100. HYPIPAMEE

Mount Hypipamee is the most unusual volcanic site the author has ever visited. It has no conical shape, no ash and scoria, no signs of lava flows and is not surrounded by volcanic soil; it's just a hole in the ground. That hole is almost cylindrical, 131m deep

and averages around 60m in diameter. Water fills slightly more than half. And furthermore, it's in solid granite!

It's the granite component that's responsible for Hypipamee's bizarre features. Granite is formed 2–12km below the surface where it cools, solidifies and crystallises. The granite in the Atherton area is over 300 million years old. That's ample time for erosion to remove the overlying rocks. As the older rocks went, pressure on the granite was reduced, allowing it to expand. As it expanded it developed fine cracks that ran both parallel and vertical to the surface (**#55**).

Sometime in the last 7 million years, volcanic activity to the east of Hypipamee forced magma (lava that has not reached the surface) into the cracks of Hypipamee's granite. These cracks also contained water which became super-heated to well over 100°C. Under such pressure, something gave way and

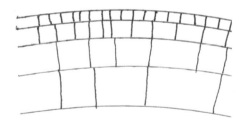

the water instantly turned to steam expanding over 2,000 fold blasting out the hole. Such holes are termed diatremes. There are no signs of lava flow, but a few samples of lava bombs have been found in the surrounding forest. Bombs are small chunks of solidified lava thrown out at the time of the eruption.

Freshwater shrimps thrive in the lake. Its surface contains patches of floating native duckweed, while the lake floor is covered by decaying vegetation. Long strings of algae hang vertically within the waters. The lake has near-constant temperature from top to bottom, which at time of testing ranged between 17.2–17.5°C. This indicates that there is constant mixing, with cold water sinking and warm water rising. This is not uncommon in small deep lakes.

Large granitic rocks (opposite page, bottom left) border the path just prior to the viewing platform. The 800m return path is bituminised and even wheelchair friendly. A steeper side track leads down to the picturesque Dinner Falls. The car park area is well serviced and contains numerous information boards.

101. ILLAWARRA ESCARPMENT

Like a riddle found in Christmas crackers: 'It's big, it's getting
bigger, but the bigger it gets, the less there is to see. What is it?'
It's the Illawarra Escarpment, a spectacular feature of the New
South Wales south coast. An escarpment is a one-sided hill.

The Illawarra Escarpment, or
simply the 'Illawarra Scarp', is a
small part of the much-fragmented
Great Escarpment that stretches
the full length of the east coast of
Australia. Around 50 million or
more years ago the land surface of
the Illawarra was at least 1,000m
above Wollongong and extended
more than 50km out to the east.
The seas and rivers that were
there at that time have removed
thousands of cubic kilometres of
rock that once filled this space.
Likewise, rivers that now drain the
land area west of Wollongong have
eroded hundreds cubic kilometres
of rock that were once in place
between the plateau cliffs and the
city.

The area between the sea
and the cliffs, the Illawarra Plain,
is wedge shaped and extends

from the narrow beach at Stanwell Park
(above) south to the elongated Saddleback
Mountain west of Kiama.

Early geologists thought the escarpment
was a retreating major north-south fault
scarp. Those thoughts were ended by coal
miners who tunnelled west from mines in
the Bulli area and under the Illawarra Scarp.

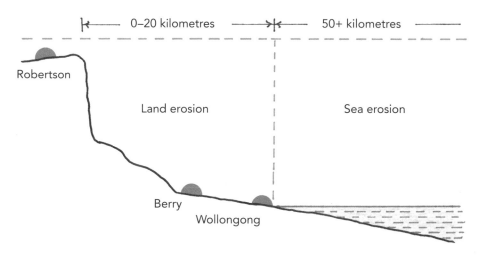

The general uplift that raised the Sydney Basin (including the Illawarra) was greatest in the east, out towards the continental 'drop over' where there are major north-south faults. Evidence for this can be viewed at Austinmer Beach adjacent to the outcropping coal seams (opposite page, bottom right). Strata on the headland are tilted ever so slightly upwards towards the east.

The cliffed scarp retreats as less resistant rock below the sandstone erodes, undercutting the Sydney Basin Sandstone. Periodically, large rock-falls occur. The one shown (below) is above Coledale.

102. INNOT HOT SPRINGS

There are two clues to tell you where the springs are. The first is
steam rising from Nettle Creek, the second, where the bathers
are. Not that the bathers will be found where the springs are;
there the water's too hot. They'll be a little further downstream
from the hot springs; at places where they can choose their own spots with their
preferred temperatures.

Photo: Shutterstock | FiledIMAGE

Upstream from the springs, all of Nettle Creek's water comes from near surface sources such as runoff and downhill seepage. The amount varies enormously from one season to the next.

The springs add additional water to this smallish stream. The springs come from deep, deep down, and they're hot, hot, hot! Around 71°C. That's hot enough to cause some parts of your body to blister.

By analysing the spring water's chemical content, geologists contend that this water would have reached temperatures above 100°C while at depths greater than 3km. The main impurity in the water is common salt (NaCl), but there are plenty of others chemicals present, such as fluoride, that induce people to use the springs as a health spa.

Once you've found water of the appropriate temperature, you scoop out a hole in the sand and lie in the warm water. The alternative is to use the facilities of the adjacent Leisure and Health Park where there are more amenities and the water is filtered.

103. JENOLAN CAVES

The road into Jenolan to inspect the world's oldest known limestone cave system is both steep and narrow, but the careful driver and tense passengers are rewarded at their destination with access to the finest of cave formations. Nine caves out of the more than 80 discovered are open to the public. But there's much to see without going underground.

Grand Arch (below) and Carlotta Arch (opposite page, top) are spectacular landforms that come into view as you enter the caves area. Grand Arch is an example of a cave formed by a stream that has gradually dissolved its way through the limestone. While Carlotta Arch is a higher arch, initially formed as a cave in a narrow limestone ridge.

The original Jenolan Limestone was laid down between 430 million and 410 million years ago. It consists of four major and a number of minor strata totalling 200m to 25m in thickness. Lying above, between and below the limestone are a series of shales, mudstones and sandstones. About 60 million to 70 million years after the formation of the limestone the whole area was compressed, folded and uplifted in the Lachlan Fold event (**#116**). It is thought that caves started to form

shortly after the uplift. Over the next 230 million years the region fell below sea level and rose again several times. While submerged, fresh limestone formed and filled or partially filled the earlier caves. About 120 million years ago the area was again lifted above sea level and has remained there ever since. The initial folding and compression fractured much of the strata, causing slopes in the limestone to vary from vertical to near-horizontal. The caves in steeply sloping areas, such as River Cave, tend to be very deep, while those in the flatter areas, the ones most visited, are more tunnel-like.

You can view the shale/slate formation that abuts the limestone by taking the Jenolan River Walk that starts at the eastern entrance to the Grand Arch. The near-vertical flaking shale/slate rock is exposed on the southern bank of the track about halfway along Blue Lake (below left). It is unusual to have such a change from one rock type to another so exposed and easily accessed. In the photo (below right), the key is resting on the shale/slate while the limestone is pavement-like at the bottom. The colouring of the clear water in Blue Lake is not true; it's caused by light refracting from the dissolved calcium carbonate held within the water.

But it's the speleothems most people come to see.

104. KAKADU ESCARPMENT

Kakadu is one of those wonderful destinations that has something
to offer to almost everyone. Its aboriginal art sites are astounding,
its 'winter' climate is warm and dry, four-wheel driving is permitted
and challenging, the animal life colourful and varied, and its scenery staggering.
Much of the tourist industry in this World-Heritage-listed national park revolves
around the escarpment where the Arnhem Plateau meets the lowland plains and
swamps.

The geologic history of this escarpment had its beginnings some 2.5 billion
years ago. At around that time granite was intruded below the surface. Over the
next billion years the Kakadu region experienced erosion, uplift and folding that
produced mountains possibly the height of Mount Kosciuszko; more erosion,
another intrusion of granite and even outpourings from volcanoes. When all this
action ceased, massive rivers eroded the mountains, and the sands and gravel they
carried were deposited on a plain that covered much of the northern half of the
Northern Territory. The accumulated sand compacted to form sandstone while
the coarser gravels formed conglomerate. Conglomerate can be seen at the foot of
the many cliffs that mark the escarpment. Where was Australia during all this time?

Twin Falls.

Photo: Stewart Barrett.

Photo: Stewart Barrett.

Just drifting around the Earth doing the normal tourist thing, but you can be 99.9 per cent sure that it wasn't anywhere near where it is now.

Around 140 million years ago and coinciding with the break-up of Gondwana, the north-eastern section of the plain began to sink. The sea invaded and covered what is now the Kakadu Plain. Ocean waves crashed into the partly submerged conglomerate, forming sea cliffs. After another 40 million years the land rose again. The Arnhem escarpment is the remains of the former sea cliffs.

The submergence and subsequent re-emergence of the sandstone and conglomerate strata was neither even, nor gentle. Deep joints (cracks) formed, running down from the surface. When the land eventually settled, air and water penetrated these joint lines. They became enlarged to form narrow ravines, and when viewed from the air have a distinct geometric pattern (above).

The escarpment (below) defines the western edge of the Arnhem Plateau and runs along the eastern boundary of the park. To the north and east, the plateau covers all the 'far top end'. Here it rises to an altitude of more than 300m. The edge of the plateau retreats by erosion undercutting the cliffs. It has been estimated that the speed of retreat is about 1m every thousand years.

105. KALGOORLIE GOLD

The mine may not be natural, but the gold certainly is. Kalgoorlie is located on one of Western Australia's mineral-rich greenstone belts. These belts are very ancient at around 2.4 billion years of age. They are the result of volcanic activity that occurred a few hundred million years after the massive injections of granite that welded and formed the Yilgarn Craton. These upswellings of magma occurred at great depths under tremendous pressure a very long time ago. Kalgoorlie's greenstone is chemically related to basalt/dolerite, but also contains significant quantities of olivine [$(Mg, Fe)_2 SiO_4$], a primary component of the Earth's upper mantle. This

greenstone rock is exposed now, only because kilometres of the prior surface have been removed by erosion. Contained within any upwelling of magma is a huge, huge volume of water. This water contains dissolved minerals, including gold, silver, lead, copper, nickel and zinc as well as many other lesser-known ones. (In 2015, reports of dissolved silver and gold being found in the water of volcanic lakes in New Zealand appeared in reputable science journals.)

The greenstone, itself an intrusion, has experienced secondary intrusions termed lodes or veins. Some of these contain commercial quantities of minerals. Similar veins and lodes may also be present in gneiss and other ancient rocks. A common intrusion is quartz (SiO_2), which sometimes (but not as often as some would wish) is accompanied by gold and silver. The quartz, silver and gold all entered the greenstone as super-heated salty water under great pressure. As the mineral-laden water moved towards the surface its pressure and temperature dropped, causing it to precipitate its mineral load. In its primary form, gold is a malleable crystal.

The specks (opposite page, left) are of secondary or alluvial gold. These gold flakes started life as fragments of primary gold, but the rocks in which they were housed have been eroded away and the gold transported from its original location, most probably by running water. The gold at Kalgoorlie is somewhat different. Although some pure gold exists, most occurs as compounds of gold and iron pyrites (fool's gold). For extraction this requires extensive crushing and various flotation processes, followed by gold cyanidation.

The super pit is 3.5km long, 1.5km wide and 600m deep.

Photos: Chris and Judy Pratt.

106. KANANGRA UNCONFORMITY

Conformity, when applied to sedimentary rocks, means that rock strata are in order of age with no gaps. The youngest are at the top with ages increasing regularly for strata beneath. Unconforming rock strata don't follow this pattern. Geologists use the term 'unconformity' specifically to indicate a gap in age between one

strata and that of the one immediately above. Such an unconformity is on view along the Kanangra Walls. Here the conforming Sydney Basin rocks deposited 300 million to 250 million years ago sit unconformably on 380-million- to 360-million-year-old Lachlan Fold Rocks (**#116**). There's a 90-million-year gap between the top of the sloping strata and the horizontally bedded Sydney Basin sandstones above.

Lachlan Fold rocks were forced up during this mountain-building period. The next 90 million years was given over to erosion that lowered and smoothed the surfaces. The area then sank below sea level and only then did the Sydney Basin begin to form. The basin gradually filled and later was uplifted. Kanangra Creek has cut a 600m-deep gorge to expose both set of rocks; the Sydney Basin on top, the line of unconformity and then the angled strata of the Lachlan Fold rocks.

The line of unconformity is spectacularly clear (above and below right), however, the angled strata are often blurred by blocks of algae covered Sydney Basin sandstones that have been undercut and fallen onto the folded rocks below.

After taking your photos of the unconformity don't move. Look down at the rock on which you are standing. Yes it's a coarse conglomerate, but

it's odd. Note the angular characteristics of its component particles (below left). This rock was laid down under the sea during an ice age. Melting, floating icebergs dropped their load hereabouts. Such rock is termed tillite.

107. KARIJINI

It's impossible to visit the Hamersley Ranges without being struck by two things: the incredible rough beauty of the place, and the immensity of the iron-mining operations. The two go hand in hand. The presence of so much iron gives the countryside its incredible red colour and the nature of the rock formations is the foundation for its stunning scenery.

The underlying strata of its Karijini and Millstream-Chichester National Parks is remarkably flat even though the surface may be undulating to hilly. This flatness indicates that the original uplift was slow, even and gentle. Most of the gorges are of relatively recent origin, beginning to form only 50 million years ago. Erosion was spurred by a combination of falling sea levels and further gentle uplift of the land. Streams cut quickly and deeply into the rock following weaknesses along joint lines. This resulted in geometrically patterned gorges with straight lines commonly terminating in angular bends. Oxers Lookout (below left) gives views over the junction of Red, Weano, Joffre and Hancock Gorges that share the intersection of four such joint lines. This lookout is a favourite among photographers. Some but not all gorges are cut into the high-iron-content strata of the Pilbara (**#166**).

Heads of many gorges are marked by waterfalls, cascades and inviting swimming holes. Such places, in geo-speak, are appropriately termed knick-points. Some spellings omit the 'k'. Their presence is an indicator of youth in the landscape and that the topography downstream may be quite different to that above the knick-point.

Fortescue Falls/Circular Pool.

Photos: Ian Boxall.

108. KATA TJUTA (THE OLGAS)

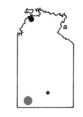

Kata Tjuta is a remnant of an ancient mountain fold – it is simply
another of a series of peaks formed during the same mountain-
building event that produced Uluru and the MacDonnell Ranges.
Uluru and Kata Tjuta are the remnants of an old folded mountain system and they
now float in a sea of sand that they helped create. The red/brown colour of the
rock is from the oxidisation of iron that was contained within the original sand and
coarse gravel.

Kata Tjuta has an entirely different shape to that of Uluru (**#204**). This rocky
outcrop consists of 28 large rounded domes and a similar number of smaller ones.
The difference in shape is due to two factors, the rock type and the slope of the strata.
Kata Tjuta is conglomerate (opposite, below) – a very resistant sedimentary rock
consisting of rounded pebbles and stones of granite and ironstone cemented
together. The inclination of its sedimentary layers is around 25° rather than the
near-vertical angles at Uluru. This makes the surface more 'normal' in that erosion
is attacking the upward-facing surface of the sedimentary rock rather than its
'ends' or 'sides'.

The surface of the Kata Tjuta block is crisscrossed by major joints that

Photo: Barbara Weiner.

account for the domed formations. Four such joints bound each dome. The joints allow water and air to penetrate deep below the surface. Weathering along these joints and subsequent erosion by water running down the bare rock has cut steep canyons into the rock formation. Erosion of extra deep and multi-fractured joints has resulted in the formation of some wider and gentler sloping canyons.

The 'Valley of the Winds' walk (above) through Kata Tjuta is popular with those wanting something more than just a quick visit to Uluru and Kata Tjuta.

109. KATHERINE GORGE (NITMILUK)

Katherine Gorge has been cut through the same Kombolgie
Formation of conglomerate and sandstone as comprises the Arnhem
Plateau. The Katherine River has cut a series of gorges, 13 in all,

through the Kombolgie
Formation following major
joint lines. The gorge also has
the same geologic history as the
southern section of Kakadu
National Park, including the
flooding of the land 140
million years ago (**#104**).

The pattern of gorges is
such that they contain many
right-angle bends as the stream
has cut from one major north-
east/south-west joint line along

a north-west/south-east line through to another major joint running parallel to the first. Small falls and rapids mark the  junctions between gorge sections and some small tributaries join the main stream by means of waterfalls. Abandoned earlier river courses contain 'dead' gorges.

In places sheer cliffs tower up to 70m above the water. The first two gorges are easily accessible by commercial tour boat or canoe. Here the cliff faces display horizontal to gently tilted bedding planes. These planes mark the break between one sedimentary series and another. Each individual series is the result of a group of flooding episodes spread over a long period of time. Undercutting by the river removes support for strata above, causing whole cliff faces to occasionally fall. Sharp edges from these falls accentuate the bedding planes. Vertical dark streaks on the cliffs are made by the growth of algae that feed on water seeps from above.

110. KEEP RIVER 'BEEHIVES'

Keep River National Park is accessed along a 30km gravel road that is unlikely to tear apart your two-wheel drive car. The sandstone formations in the Keep River National Park are fascinating for their shapes, colours and composition.

One common stratum you will notice is conglomerate (opposite, top left). Conglomerate looks like a poor batch of coarse concrete. Some of the individual stones within this conglomerate have diameters in excess of 50mm. This indicates that they were carried to their position by very fast flowing water at or near the coast. Other strata (opposite, top right) composed of very fine grains of sand may lie above or below the conglomerate, demonstrating that they were laid down in relatively still water some distance from shore. Such differences in pebble and sand grain sizes, and distances from the coast, are indications of widely fluctuating climates and sea levels 200 million years ago.

Soft or poorly cemented layers have crumbled and eroded away. In these isolated rock outcrops along the Goorrandalng Circuit (opposite, centre and below), near-horizontal weak strata have eroded to develop tunnel windows that run from one side of the ridge/outcrop through to the other.

111. KEILOR ROSETTE ROCK

Rosette Rock is located in the Victorian Organ Pipes National Park. The pipes may be prominent and have the naming rights to this small park, but it is Rosette Rock that claims my attention.

It is thought that Rosette Rock, Organ Pipes and Tessellated Pavement are quite young; less than 5 million years old. Jackson Creek has cut down through a lava flow to expose its basalt cooling columns (Organ Pipes), Tessellated Pavement and

Rosette Rock. The radiating columns of the rosette are thought to have formed in an empty, cold lava tube like those at Undara (**#205**) in Queensland and the Harman Valley in Victoria (**#28**). Fresh lava flowed into and filled the tube. As this lava was not exposed to the air, cooling did not take place from the top, but from all round its circumference (**#70**). The thin, wedge-shaped cracking pattern developed around that circumference and gradually spread to the last part of the flow to cool its centre. If you stand back and look at the rosette you can see the cylindrical shape of the filled lava tube running back into the valley walls.

The Tessellated Pavement is simply the tops of the same columns as exposed at the Organ Pipes. They're just a little further upstream and have had their tops eroded by Jackson Creek.

Tessellated Pavement.

Organ Pipes.

112. KELLY HILL CAVES

Kangaroo Island is a fascinating place whether you are a geologist, biologist, zoologist or just a plain nature lover. I put geologist first because it's Kangaroo Island's rocks that give it such diversity. Kangaroo Island is closely related to the Flinders and Mount Lofty Ranges. That explains the presence of granite, 500-million-year-old red sandstone and some even older contorted rock formations. But it's not all old. The limestone and much of the sand is very young, dating from the last ice ages less than 2 million years ago. And it is in this juvenile limestone that Kelly Caves have formed.

There's a certain sameness about limestone caves that leaves some casual visitors bored, but this cave has something extra. First of all, it's not really in limestone, it's in calcarenite – a proto-limestone derived from limestone sand. The calcarenite sand formed as a dune more than 500,000 years ago during the last ice ages. The dune is gradually cementing itself together and if left undisturbed in the future will eventually form mature limestone.

Normally caves in limestone are formed from the top down. Acidic water seeps from the ground above and in doing so dissolves the limestone and eventually forms caves. At Kelly Hill the acidic water came in from below. A swamp at the ground-level edge of the dune leaked acidic water into the base of the dune, gradually dissolving channels through the dune. As the channels enlarged, portions of the sandy roof collapsed, further expanding the channels and forming a network of caves. The second stage of development occurred with the stabilising of the dunes by the growth of trees, grasses and shrubs on the surface. Rotting vegetation caused rainwater seeping through the dune surface from above to become acidic. That then began to dissolve the now lightly cemented lime sand from above and led to the growth of straws and stalactites hanging from the caves' roofs. The porosity of the calcarenite causes water to enter the cave roof via a multitude of channels, resulting in an incredible density of roof decorations. There are, of course, the usual flow stones and stalagmites to be found on the cave floor.

With Kelly Hill Caves' geologic history, it's not surprising that the cave floor is flat with little need for stairs.

113. KIAMA BLOWHOLE

The blowhole is brilliant when the sea is just right – a heavy swell coming in from the south-east – but can be disappointing if the sea is being less co-operative.

There is more to a good blowhole than just a tunnel-like cave with a hole in the roof. It's all about the plumbing. Blowholes work best if the hole is back from the end of the tunnel, as it is at Kiama. Water flows in through the mouth of the tunnel, completely filling the front of the tunnel, and surges towards the end of the blowhole. As the surge passes the blowhole, some surge will splash up the sides but most, still filling the tunnel, will move forward towards the tunnel's end. The air at the end becomes highly compressed (**A**). It is this compressed air that stops the momentum of the water, not the end of the tunnel.

In Kiama's case, more than 200 tonnes of water may move into the tunnel. Once forward motion has ceased the water would normally drain back towards the entrance. Getting hundreds of tonnes of water to turn around and go into reverse is rather slow. But then, there's that compressed air at the end which is now trying to escape! It blows the water out through the blowhole as the quickest way to decompress the tunnel (**B**). The power of the escaping compressed air can force water more than 50m into the air and totally drench unsuspecting bystanders.

The blowhole without the blow (below right), and blowing with vigour (opposite).

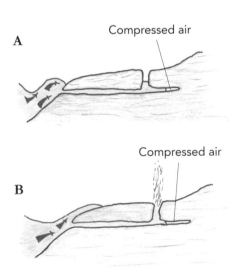

114. KINGS CANYON

Kings Canyon is much more than a spectacular 100m-high red sandstone cliff rising above a strip of green trees in a desert. It's an exhibition place showcasing central Australia's most outstanding geologic features. The 3–4-hour canyon rim walk is one of the finest and most rewarding short walks in Australia.

South-west-facing cliff.

The canyon's spectacular cliffs were formed in 360-million-year-old Mereenie Sandstone. In the period from 340 million to 310 million years ago, major mountain building to the north caused the area around Kings Canyon to rise to a position well above sea level – a position it has held ever since. Although there was no massive folding in the area, the uplift caused the Mereenie Sandstone to crack and form joints. The rectangular patterned joint lines determine the orientation of the canyon rim's main features. Its beehives are a similar shape to those in the Bungle Bungles of Western Australia (**#173**), but without the bold stripes. There's very little clay in the rock to hold water and/or sand grains together in this sandstone. The stripes on these rocks simply mark each individual stratum as it has been

deposited. The joints allowed water and air to penetrate, and commence the removal, grain by grain, of the rock between the joints. Both wind and rain have been major eroders over the past 20 million years. Exposed surface grains in the sandstone become loose as they oxidise or when moisture weakens the cement that holds them together. Infrequent storms lash the bare surface and wash out the cracks.

The spectacular main canyon has formed along a major joint line with the creek eroding a deep valley with vertical walls on both sides at its head. The north-facing wall has developed a veneer of red to orange desert varnish that has protected much of it from weathering. Desert varnish is a thin film of iron, manganese and other similar oxides that form on the surface. Water percolating through the sandstone has carried these minerals to the surface of the canyon wall. As the surface dries the oxides remain, forming a face highly resistant to weathering either by air or water. Pockets of cavernous weathering (below) affect parts of the south-west-facing wall where salt accumulation has weakened the desert varnish. Cavernous weathering (tafoni) is common in granular rocks such as sandstone and granite located in deserts or coastal situations. In these areas salt is common and may accumulate on a rocky surface. Rain and dew can dissolve this

salt and percolate between the rock's grains. Later, as the water evaporates, the salt will crystallise and force grains of rock loose from the surface. The south-west-facing wall has been subject to more active erosion and hence had less time to develop this protective varnish.

115. KOSCIUSZKO'S PATTERNED LAND

Patterned land is rare, particularly in Australia. It is restricted
to tundra areas of the world and is associated with periglacial
climates. Periglacial is almost glacial. It has temperatures in winter continually
below 0°C and weeks or many days in spring and autumn fluctuating between
below and above 0°C. Summer weeks frequently rise above 0°C. Most studies
into patterned land have been undertaken in the tundra soils of the northern
hemisphere and conclude that patterning there is mainly the result of frost
wedging. Frost wedging also occurs on Kosciuszko, but there's no soil on this site.
Best look for another solution.

This patterning is the result of its plants and the site's specific physical features.
These plants are termed feldmark flora. They grow in rocky areas of little or no
soil and in climatic conditions outlined above. Where there is slope and a huge

range of rock sizes, as photographed (right and below), the plants appear randomly dispersed, but where it is near flat and the rocks somewhat even in size, the plant communities form clumps as in the photograph (opposite). All photos were taken from the Main Range Track between Club Lake and Lake Albina (**#148**).

The flat site is on the crest of the Great Divide. No matter the wind direction this area is blasted. And with no higher land close by, there is no seepage. Due to summer dry periods lasting for weeks, plants have had to adopt desert-plant survival strategies by growing long tentacle-like roots that extend beyond their above-ground structures. Bare rocky tracks between the clumps are a no-man's land where roots compete for available water and nutrients. Other examples of patterned land are adjacent to the track running from Thredbo Chairlift to Rawson's Pass. Parts of this track are elevated boardwalks built to protect feldmark flora.

116. LACHLAN FOLD BELT

Australia

Antarctica

The Lachlan Folding Event, mentioned in a number of sites, was the second of three major accumulation periods along the continent's east coast between 550 million and 200 million years ago.

The Delamerian, close to the Victoria/South Australia border, was the first. The second was the Lachlan/Thomson that formed most of Victoria, New South Wales and south-west Queensland, while the third, the New England, gives us the coastal areas north from Port Macquarie to the central coast of Queensland. The Lachlan and Thompson were really the same event, but the name Thompson is used to delineate the Queensland portion.

Original rocks of the Lachlan Folds form the current surface of the area depicted on the map (below). To the west they lie hidden below the Murray/Darling sediments. To the east they are covered by rocks of the Sydney Basin, while along the coast north from Port Macquarie they adjoin rocks of the younger New England Folds.

Additions to the continent were transported via mantle currents that saw the ocean floor to the east moved towards Australia and subducted beneath it in the same manner as the Pacific Ocean floor subducts beneath New Zealand, the Philippines, Taiwan and Japan today. The ocean floor, being basalt, was heavy and slid below the lightweight Australia. However, the sedimentary rocks sitting on the ocean floor were light. They resisted being pulled down and instead were scraped off against the pre-existing eastern coast. Prior to the first period of scraping, present-day Broken Hill was probably near the coast. As further scrapings were added, the east coast gradually grew eastward. As the continent's edge progressed eastward, the ocean floor was also forced to commence subducting earlier.

With thousands and thousands of repetitions of

this process along different parts of the east coast and at different times from Port Douglas in Queensland to Antarctica, area was added to the continent. The ex-sedimentary layers thousands of metres thick scraped from the ocean floor were forced into mainly north-south mountain ranges thousands of metres high separated by parallel structural valleys that often fell well below sea level. Most of these ranges have been eroded away, but numerous stumps can still be seen, as in a Hume Highway road cutting just south of Goulburn (above). Erosion quickly eroded the high and fractured mountains and deposition filled most of the large sunken areas between the ranges.

The name 'Lachlan' comes from the river of the same name that rises just north of Canberra and runs west then south to eventually drain into the Murrumbidgee.

117. LADY MUSGRAVE ISLAND

Lady Musgrave Island is a curved triangular-shaped coral cay with an area of 14ha and a surrounding reef of nearly 1,200ha. Its deep lagoon has a circumference of 8km.

There are a number of similar cays readily accessible to travellers, but Lady Musgrave Island has some distinct advantages, particularly for those coming from the south. It's at the southern end of the Great Barrier Reef and it's not overtly touristy. The only permanent infrastructure on the island is a lighthouse and a

composting toilet. Tour operators maintain a pontoon anchored in the lagoon. The pontoon is a useful base for snorkelers and divers. It is claimed that the cay's lagoon is the only one on the reef with a deep navigable entrance. This allows tour

craft to deliver you right into its heart.

The main reason for Lady Musgrave Cay's survival from cyclonic storms is the protection it gains by having beach rock around its edges. Beach rock is created by a chemical reaction between sediment and dead coral. It is initiated by the alternating

wetting and drying of the rock as tides rise and fall. Beach rock (top and left) sets like concrete and protects most of the coral sand beneath. The rock is commonly 10–50cm thick and from 2–10m wide around much of the cay's coast.

118. LAKE CAVE

Look carefully at the photo (below left) of a feature in Lake Cave in the Margaret River District of Western Australia. Yes it's a reflection, but study it a little closer. Note that there is a gap

between the two columns and their reflections in the lake water. And what does this mean? It means that if you get down low enough on the boardwalk, you can see clear through the gap between the columns' bases and the water surface.

This is the most exquisite cave formation the author has ever seen: the Suspended Table. The table is held above the water by two magnificent columns that cling tenaciously to the roof. The complete formation weighs in at 4–5 tonnes. Its evolution is quite simple, but relies upon coincidences.

The two columns each began as stalactites hanging from the roof, with matching stalagmites growing up from a flat dry floor until they joined, forming twin columns.

At the same time a thin flowstone developed on the floor between and around the columns. Later a lake formed, covering the cave floor and possibly rising partway up the columns.

The floor's surface of calcarenite (immature limestone) was dissolved to a depth of around 1m by the slightly acidic water flowing slowly through the lake. This left the calcite columns hanging. The lake surface then fell to below the bottom of the columns and the flowstone, creating this stunning formation.

That aside, Lake Cave is a beautiful cave. It's termed a 'wet' cave as its formations are actively growing from the abundant water with its dissolved calcium carbonate dripping through the roof and from stalactites and straws. The use of artistically placed lighting and reflections in the lake certainly enhance the cave's appearance.

119. LAKE EYRE

Lake Eyre covers an area of 9,500 square kilometres with its bed 15m below sea level. When the lake is dry, the salt crust has an average depth of slightly less than half a metre. When the lake is full of water the salt is dissolved and the lake has a degree of saltiness much greater than that of the Dead Sea. As the water evaporates the salt level increases

to saturation point, that is, to a point where the water is no longer capable of holding any more salt in solution. As evaporation continues, salt crystals form on the surface of the water and around the lake's edges. Eventually all the water evaporates and the layer of salt is left lying on top of a layer of mud. Each successive flood brings with it additional salt that is added to the 400 million tons already there. The small ridges of salt that develop on the crusted surface are the result of wind blowing thin plates of salt against one another at the evaporation stage when the lake has a salty crust, but liquid water beneath.

It's not strictly correct to refer to the lake as ever being full. It could only be termed full at the point where it overflowed a divide that either allowed water to flow to the sea or into another basin. If that point is ever to be reached the lake would have to be many times larger than it is today. During the massive flood of

1974 the water reached a maximum depth of 5.7m. Floods of this size are expected twice each century while minor flooding occurs every five to ten years on average.

Left: Salt-tolerant plants at the edge of Lake Eyre.

Photo: Ian Boxall

120. LAKE GEORGE

While driving south along the Federal Highway towards Canberra, and just past some of the cool-climate wineries, you may come upon a large lake 25km long and 10km wide. On the other hand you may not. Whether you do, or do not, does not depend on how much sampling you did of the Riesling or Chardonnay. This lake, Lake George – shown in 2021 (opposite) and in 2006 (below) – actually disappears and reappears on an irregular cycle. It is a result of the natural damming of a Yass River tributary following uplift along the Lake George Fault.

The Lake George Fault became active about 15 million years ago when east-west crustal pressures began to force down the land to the east of the fault. This fault is much older than Lake George and may date back even to the formation of the Lachlan Fold Belt. The pressure

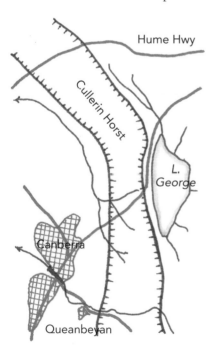

and subsequent downward movement continued intermittently until around 5 million years ago. During that time the area was sometimes a lake, sometimes a swamp and sometimes dry land. Periodic flooding by the Yass River tributary led to the surrounding land being covered by a build-up of alluvial sand, soil and gravel in the lake area. The creek, however, continued flowing south and then west to join the Yass River.

It was not until about 5 million years ago that the land between the Lake George Fault and another fault to the west, the Queanbeyan Fault, began to rise. The rising land blocked the tributary from flowing into the Yass River and in doing so formed Lake George. The land continued to rise, lifting

the original tributary channel to a point well above that of the current lake bed. The Federal Highway climbs out from the lake shore at Geary's Gap, the tributary's original course and the site for two viewing points. Turn east (left if heading towards Canberra) into the prime Weereewa Lookout, or west (right) into a slightly lower viewing point that has picnic and toilet facilities.

If you wish to see the remains of Geary's Creek (right), head towards the lower viewing point. Almost immediately a gravel road, Hadlow Drive, goes left. Follow this for 100m, turn onto Ridge Road and park. This is it. The water sits here trying to decide whether to flow east or west. It's the top of the Great Dividing Range.

121. LAKE MACQUARIE

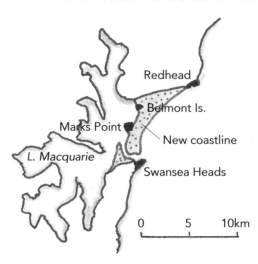

This popular body of water isn't really a lake, and it's not a river estuary. So what is it? It's a bay. Elsewhere in this book most commentary is in terms of millions or hundreds of millions of years, but not this bay. It's only a few thousand years old. The Aborigines had established themselves in Australia well before this lake was formed. Lake Macquarie and its siblings –

Lake Illawarra, Tuggerah Lakes, Myall Lakes and Wallis Lake – were all formed as the last ice age ended. Sea levels had fallen by as much as 130m during the coldest periods, then rose by the same amount by the end of the glaciation. The rising water drowned the pre-existing coast. As none of the 'lakes' have depths of anywhere near 130m, they were obviously dry land just 15,000 years ago.

By about 9,000 years ago, Macquarie Bay was a broad bay with a 10km-wide opening to the Pacific Ocean stretching from Swansea Heads in the south to Redhead in the north. Two rocky islands, Marks (Point) and Belmont, lay between these two headlands.

Swansea, Lake Macquarie, from Bolton Point.

There was no dominant Swansea Channel and the tide had three broad entry/exit points to/from the bay.

As sea level rose gradually, the sandy beaches that had developed along the ice age coast were pushed west (landward), by constructive waves. Large open bays formed as flattish land was flooded in the Illawarra and Central Coast regions. Beaches began to form across the entrances to these bays at the same time that they were being flooded.

Constructive waves break forward, stir up some sand and carry it forward up the beach. Once the wave has stopped its forward motion, most of the wave's water percolates down into the beach and the sand, that was in motion, is deposited (**#84**).

Opposite: Blacksmiths Beach stretching north from the Swansea Breakwater.

122. LAKE MUNGO

Like many of Australia's inland lakes, Mungo is a lake in name only. It probably last contained permanent water 15,000 or more years ago towards the end of the last ice age. Mungo is one of the five larger and fourteen smaller dry lakes that comprise the World Heritage-listed Willandra Creek Conservation Area. During the cold stages of the ice ages, winter snow blanketed much of the Great Dividing Range south from Toowoomba in Queensland. During spring and early summer, flooded streams flowing west from the Divide carried huge quantities of clay, silt, sand and gravel to deposit them on the already flat western plains. During flood times the streams meandered over the area, sometimes abandoning their old courses by more than 100km before cutting new ones through the easily eroded alluvial deposits.

Willandra Creek is an ana-branch of the Lachlan River. An ana-branch is a stream that leaves its parent river, runs its own course, only to rejoin the original stream at a point further downstream. Willandra Creek flooded large sections of its course, forming a series of lakes. During the wet periods these lakes were permanently full of fresh water teeming with fish and waterbirds. Abundant native animals populated the surrounding treed grasslands. It is no wonder that Aboriginal peoples selected the Mungo area as a place to live, fish and hunt.

As the climate became warmer and drier, the lakes became intermittent and increasingly salty; full in early summer, but dry by autumn. While many Aboriginal people remained in the Lake Mungo district, others were forced to migrate to other, more reliable food and water supplies. These drier conditions favoured the development of the sand dune now known as The Walls of China (opposite, below). Mungo Lake, when full, had an irregular oval shape, and was approximately 20km long, 10km wide and 15m deep. Sandy beaches ringed it and trees grew around its edge and on the surrounding alluvial plain. Prevailing westerly and south-westerly winds blew the sand to the eastern and north-eastern shores of the lake where the sand became trapped in the trees and formed a continuous dune. This dune was crescent shaped as it paralleled the lake's edge.

Dunes of this shape and formed in this manner are termed lunettes. As the climate dried further and water levels fell, the lakebed of clay, fine silt and salt was increasingly exposed. This fine material was carried by the wind and caught by the vegetation and the sand dune, covering both to varying depths. The clay solidified and anchored the lunette into a stationary position. Scientists estimate that the lake has been dry for at least 15,000 years.

Above: Mungo lakebed. Below: Walls of China.

123. LATROBE VALLEY'S BROWN COAL

You don't expect to find a brown-coal mine featured in a nature
book, but it has its place. Not because of the mining, but because
of what the mining reveals. Brown coal is as natural as trees. Brown coal's technical
name is lignite; it's a combustible, soft sedimentary rock. Brown coal is the second
stage in the formation of bituminous (black) and anthracite coals. The first stage is
the development of peat.

Australia ranks fourth in the mining of lignite behind Germany, Russia and the
USA. Its deposits, however, are huge. The Latrobe Valley contains 25 per cent of
the world's brown coal – far more than is found in any other region or country.

The brown coal started forming as peat around 50 million years ago and
continued on for the next 35 million years. Peat is an accumulation of dead
vegetation that has failed to rot away due to a shortage of oxygen within the
decaying material. The climate was temperate and moist, and the vegetation lush;
so we can conclude that the area must have been swampy. The Latrobe Valley area
subsided, but the growing thickness of peat kept pace with the subsidence. The
subsidence was probably caused by the Earth's crust stretching and thinning as
Australia broke free from Antarctica. The added weight of the layers of peat and
lignite would have further assisted in the subsidence. Around 10 million years ago
the area began to dry out and the brown coal covered by layers of sand and soil.
Lower sea levels then further aided in its drying out.

Overburden covering the coal varies mainly between 10–20m. A 300m-deep
borehole drilled at Morwell passed through 270m of brown coal. The deeper the
coal the more expensive it is to extract. For this reason many mines have been
enlarged by an outward spread rather than by any increase in depth.

124. LAWN HILL'S TUFA DAMS

There are other gorges in Queensland that are equally beautiful
and relaxing; so why come to this one? For some it's the
challenge of getting there, but for most it's the extras that come
with it – great scenery, great walks to suit all levels of fitness,
good campground, excellent other accommodation, varied dining options, on-site
canoe and cycle hire and poor phone reception. Lawn Hill is a wonderful place
that, as well as all the above, contains some lesser-known gems such as tufa dams.

Fed by springs emerging from upstream limestone, Lawn Hill Creek flows
continuously through this area even during the annual winter drought. For those
interested in seeing geology in the making, take the easy stroll along the Cascades
Track. It leads you across a small spring-fed tributary of Lawn Hill Creek. After
walking for about 15 minutes along the shady track you reach the Cascades. They
may be gently flowing rather than cascading, but what is really interesting are the
small delicate dams of calcium carbonate (limestone) formed across the creek
about 50m upstream from the Cascades.

The porous rocky material termed tufa (pronounced 'toofa') grows at up to
25mm a year. Its formation has some similarity to the growth of speleothems in
limestone caves. Super-saturated calcium carbonate water flowing from springs
loses some of its carbon dioxide (CO_2) on exposure to the open air.

This reduction is accelerated by shallow turbulent water as it flows over
and around rocks. As the CO_2 levels fall the water's capacity to hold calcium
carbonate ($CaCO_3$) also falls. Deposition builds outwards and upwards from
exposed surfaces and results in the formation of low dams, as found above the
Cascades. The dam's brownish colour results from the presence of dissolved iron
in the water and a surface covering of algae and moss. Tufa is very soft and easily
damaged by foot traffic. Light, refracting through the same calcium carbonate
that builds the tufa, is also responsible for the green colour of the water. Calcium
carbonate concentrations in the main gorge are well below those of some of its
tributary creeks.

125. LITCHFIELD'S TERMITE MOUNDS

It's the Magnetic Termite mounds that attract the most scientific interest. These broad, thin mounds are aligned with the thin ends facing north–south. This architecture benefits the termites (*Amitermes meridionalis*) by always having one major side of their home in shade. But how do the termites know direction, particularly as the mounds are constructed by

blind workers? Scientists thought that it may be due to the termite having an in-built compass. To test this theory, scientists cancelled the normal north magnetic tug by placing strong magnets to the east and west of termite mounds. The workers immediately commenced enlarging their mound to their new east–west magnetic pull, thus proving the theory to be correct.

Termite mounds are great for dress-up parties. They're also of real interest to scientists.

The other termite mounds of interest belong to a different group of termites whose architects have

opted for the 'bigger is better' approach to keeping themselves comfortable.

Only a small amount of each mound type extends below ground level. This is because the water table here is shallow and during the wet season the whole area becomes a shallow lake. The termites' main food is dry grass which is collected by the workers and stored in the mounds. Foraging takes place mainly of an evening and night as the termite's body is thin skinned and easily damaged by direct sunlight.

The Cathedral Termites (*Nasutitermes triodiae*) build massive mounds, many of which exceed 5m in height.

126. LONDON BRIDGE (NSW)

London Bridge is a limestone arch over Burra Creek – a minor tributary of the Queanbeyan River. The limestone was deposited before the big squeeze that resulted in the creation of the Lachlan Fold Belt (**#116**). It was also prior to the elevation of the old sea floor that now forms much of the Canberra landscape.

The steeply inclined limestone lies between equally inclined strata of compressed platy shales and mudstones. Burra Creek ran around the end of this ridge – about 200m to the east and to the left in the photo (left) – until an estimated 20,000 years ago. By that time, slightly acidic water from the surface and Burra Creek had seeped through cracks in the limestone, dissolving sufficient rock to form discontinuous cave systems. Note the small and large blind caves above the creek in the photo (below right).

Eventually a continuous cave system formed through the ridge, allowing the stream to take its present, more direct course.

Downstream, loose from the shackles of limestone, the creek enjoys the greater freedom provided by the softer shales and mudstones. Its banks are gentler, and the valley wider.

127. LONDON BRIDGE (VIC)

'London Bridge is falling down, falling down, falling down.
London Bridge is falling down, my fair Lady.' So goes the
traditional old English nursery rhyme. Well it seems to be true.
This, one of three Australian London Bridges I have visited, is
literally 'falling down.' There were formerly two arches (bottom image) but one fell
down in 1990 (below), stranding two tourists who had to be rescued by helicopter.

Most of the rock here is limestone, but the tunnels that form the arches are not
the result of common slow chemical erosion by acidic water dissolving limestone.
This was brute force. Waves pound these cliffs on average once every 15 seconds.
That's 240 times per hour. In a year it's more than 2 million times, and this has
been going on for thousands of years. All this time Bass Strait storm waves have
been hurling boulders, stones and sand at this part of the coast, tearing away at the
weakest points.

The 1990 collapse was simply a case of gravity versus rock. Gravity won.

Gravity always wins whether it be arches
or undercut cliffs. If you come back to
visit in 100 years time – that more than
200 million waves later – London Bridge
may have completely fallen down with
nothing to show that it was once even
there. However, there may be a new one
somewhere else along the coast.

128. LONDON BRIDGE (WA)

Western Australia's London Bridge is found outside the small
town of Sandstone. The town's name is a false clue when trying to
fathom the bridge's geology. Sandstone's London Bridge has been
constructed from basalt, which is a common volcanic rock. Again, there's very
little in the bridge that looks like basalt – there's no black colour and there are no
columns.

This basalt is 350 million years old. Where its source volcano was located,
I don't know. The bridge was built from a basalt lava flow. The chief processes
involved in its formation were chemical weathering and laterisation. Over time the
basalt has chemically weathered, breaking down to its basic particles of clay, iron,
phosphates and other bits and pieces. This weathering is caused by the composite
particles of basalt reacting with oxygen and water, resulting in the formation of
saprolite (opposite, below).

Laterisation has then changed the saprolite (**#165**) by the same process that
built the breakaways (**#20**) and similar landforms. Laterisation occurs in wet–dry
climates and in the presence of iron. The process sees surface and near-surface
particles resorted by vertical movements. In the wet season, clay particles and
dissolved salts are both carried down. In the dry season the dissolved salts are
returned to the surface by capillary action. These salts are then washed away in the
next rains. Iron and aluminium oxides are not readily dissolved and so remain at or
near the surface. With the removal of the other minerals, the iron and aluminium
oxides cement themselves together forming a hard and resistant surface. This
resistant surface forms the arch of London Bridge; the softer material beneath
has been removed by water and wind erosion. Note the presence of iron (rusty
red) and clay (white) in the photo (opposite, below), which was taken further along
the same ridge, with the line between the laterite (top half) and the saprolite being
quite sharp.

129. LOST CITY, CAPE CRAWFORD

Although nearly 600km apart, this Lost City and the one at Litchfield have much in common. Both are in uplifted horizontally bedded sandstone and both have tower structures defined by a weathered checkerboard pattern of vertical joint lines. This Lost City is in the Caranbirini Conservation Reserve, 64km north-east of Cape Crawford, along the Carpentaria Highway.

The Caranbirini towers are up to 25m high and are made more attractive by their pancake-like appearance. Each 'pancake' marks a separate depositional episode. Flood events at Caranbirini involved a large river that flowed into a shallow sea. Each flood was generally marked by coarse material being deposited at the beginning and finer material at the end of each flood. The junction between different flooding events is termed a bedding plane. Differences in the resistance to erosion by adjacent beds lead to each stratum being accentuated as a 'pancake'.

Evidence for the sea being shallow comes from fallen rocks including this one (bottom left). The now upright rock's bedding plane shows ripple marks similar to those found today in shallow water. The colouring is from different sources. The greys and blacks are not stains but algal growth, while the red/orange is from iron contained within the sandstone that oxidised (rusted) with exposure to air.

There are no facilities at the Caranbirini Conservation Reserve so it's vitally important to bring a good supply of water. You may stay longer than you first expected.

130. LOST CITY, LITCHFIELD

Of all the 'Lost Cities' in the NT, I find this one the most to my
liking. It has touches of Inca stonework reminiscent of Machu
Picchu, Peru, combined with elements of Stonehenge, UK.

The 9km road into the Lost City is declared 'FOUR-WHEEL DRIVE ONLY';
and it is. But I did notice several beaten-up old town cars in its parking lot.

Many of the vertical joints in the sandstone here have been eroded to narrow
slits and alleys while the bedding planes are close to horizontal. The main strata are
each a 0.5–1.0m thick, making the pillars appear like carefully laid blocks placed
one on top of the other. The older, darker colouring is from algae, while the
brighter yellows and oranges are oxidised iron weeping from seepages on more
recently exposed faces.

The shortish track around the site is reasonably flat. There is ample parking
space, but no other facilities.

131. LOWBIDGEE FLOODPLAIN

'Lowbidgee' is a common abbreviation for the Lower Murrumbidgee Floodplain – an area lying between the Lachlan and Murrumbidgee Rivers at their fractured confluence. The Lachlan splits into a number of distributary creeks that individually flow into the Murrumbidgee. The overall flat region is broken by stabilised sand dunes and strings of intermittent lakes.

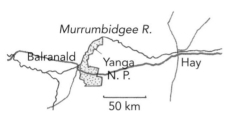

Inhabited by Aboriginal peoples for at least 40,000 years, the region was first settled by Europeans in the early 1840s. An early landholder was William C Wentworth, the Blue Mountains explorer, who established Yanga Station surrounding Yanga Lake near Balranald. Other than for the addition of sheep, homesteads and fences, the landscape remained relatively unchanged up until the end of the 1800s. In the early 20th century human-made changes to river flows started, then accelerated. Weirs were built to facilitate river transport, diversions to aid irrigation upstream from Narrandera, and huge storage dams constructed on the Lachlan, Murrumbidgee and Murray Rivers. The disruption to the natural flow of water through Lowbidgee was devastating for birds, native animals and River Red Gums. Now, in the 21st century, changes are being made to partially restore the natural rhythm of the water flow.

The present landforms and residual vegetation developed as the last ice ages ended 15,000–12,000 years ago. The land had been drier then. Sandhills, similar to those at Lake Mungo (**#122**), formed on what was already a multi-million-year-old flood plain. The flood plain consisted of coalescing and shifting inland deltas, laid on top of one another. Such deltas are referred to as alluvial fans. A vertical cut through these deposits would reveal a mishmash of clay, dust, ash, sand, old lake beds and prior river courses.

Surviving lakes and permanent rivers are fringed by River Red Gums, which in turn are hemmed in by hardy saltbush perennials. All is green following a wet season. Yanga is now a national park.

132. LYNDHURST OCHRE PITS

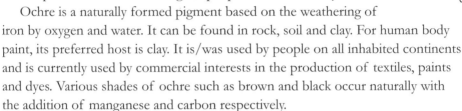

What colour would you like? This must have been like a giant colour DIY supermarket for the Aboriginal peoples of the Lake Eyre Basin.

Ochre is a naturally formed pigment based on the weathering of iron by oxygen and water. It can be found in rock, soil and clay. For human body paint, its preferred host is clay. It is/was used by people on all inhabited continents and is currently used by commercial interests in the production of textiles, paints and dyes. Various shades of ochre such as brown and black occur naturally with the addition of manganese and carbon respectively.

Aboriginal men currently, and in the past, travelled up to hundreds of kilometres to dig and collect this high-grade ochre. Some of the ochre was collected for personal use, but much was traded for other goods and services. The startling pits are accessed by a short gravel road that leaves the Lyndhurst to Marree road about 5km north of Lyndhurst.

133. MACKENZIE DRIVE

Most of New England's national parks lie along the forested high-rainfall eastern edge of the huge New England granite mass. Many of these parks are remote and serviced only by minor roads. But Tenterfield's Mackenzie Drive traverses the same granite, lies west of a major town and just off the New England Highway. The land here is flatter and drier and mainly used for grazing sheep and cattle. The area is popular with sapphire, diamond and gold prospectors as well as granite junkies.

An A4 mud map and description of the drive is available free from the local Information Office on the main street. The drive is 38km long and begins and ends with sealed roads, but is mainly on well-kept gravel suitable for all motorised vehicles. Interesting features you should look for include large exposed areas of granite where near-horizontal cracks (joint lines) in the rock run almost parallel to the surface (**#55**). In the photo (below) the joint lines slope down slightly left to right. These weathered and eroded joints are the result of the granite expanding upward as the weight of overlying rock was reduced as they eroded away.

There are numerous beautifully shaped and balancing rocks to be seen on the circuit, but my favourite is a lone boulder neatly split into three segments. Not only do masses of granite expand when pressure is reduced (opposite, above) – individual boulders also retain those same pressures and when relieved of constrictions, they also split.

134. MACQUARIE MARSHES

This is not your usual tourist destination. Who wants to visit a swamp for their annual vacation? But some nature-loving people do. There's not a great range of accommodation – there are few roads and it's a long way from anywhere.

The Macquarie Marshes is on a flood plain – part of the huge flood plain that is at the heart of the Murray–Darling Basin. The rock underneath is irrelevant. It's the alluvial mud on top that makes it what it is. The Macquarie River for millions of years has been carrying silt from its headwaters on the Western Slopes and dropping it where the river's slope and speed drop to almost zero. The Macquarie here becomes a braided stream – one where distributaries leave the main channel only to rejoin further downstream or run into other distributaries, or even into other rivers which are running parallel. In many ways the marshes are like a delta, but they're different in that all the distributaries eventually come back together to reform as an ordinary river.

The image (below left) shows the Macquarie River at Dubbo, 150km upstream from the marshes. Now look at the same river near the Willie Retreat resort close to the centre of the marshes (below right). Both photos were taken on the same day.

You normally expect a river to increase in size as it moves downstream, but not the Macquarie. Some water has been lost to irrigation, but the main reason for its shrinking is its loss of water to its numerous distributaries. The marshes extend from the Marebone Weir, about 70km north of Warren, for approximately 100km along the Macquarie River to near Carinda. The marshes area is mainly 30–40km wide.

135. MADURA PASS

To the north, east and west of the Eucla sand dunes is a solid rocky limestone escarpment that rises almost 70m above the plain. The presence and orientation of the escarpment is responsible for the formation of the dunes (**#69**). The Eyre Highway climbs from the low Roe Plain to the higher Nullarbor Plain via Madura Pass.

The rocks that lay beneath the Roe Plain and those in the escarpment are one and the same – variations of the Nullarbor Limestone (**#25**) laid down on the sea floor 30 million to 20 million years ago. The Roe Plain, although limestone, is very different. It is three- to four-million-year-old calcarenite (immature limestone). This poorly cemented limestone sand contains identifiable fragments of shells – mainly oysters and bryozoans – and is only 1–3m deep.

Looking from the top of Madura Pass to the Roe Plain below.

The escarpment is a simple, but elevated, sea cliff. Following uplift, the Southern Ocean attacked this part of the continent forming the cliffs and an extensive wave-cut platform. In a period of slightly higher sea levels the calcarenite was laid down on top of the older platform.

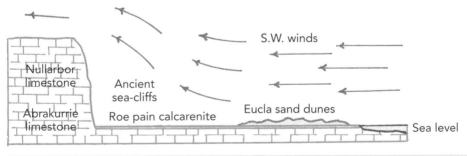

Nullarbor limestone

Ancient sea-cliffs

S.W. winds

Abrakurrie limestone

Roe pain calcarenite

Eucla sand dunes

Sea level

136. MARBLE BAR

Marble Bar – a town in the Pilbara – is best known for its high summer temperatures. Back in the 1920s, commencing 31 October 1923 and for 160 consecutive days until 7 April 1924, its maximum daily temperature never dropped below 100°F (37.8°C). The town's name, however, comes from a nearby exposed vein of rock that was first thought to be pink-red marble but eventually proved to be jasper.

Photos: Chris and Judy Pratt.

Jasper is an impure form of quartz – a common mineral formed by a combination of silicon and oxygen. Jasper's colouring is derived by the addition of iron to the mixture. Quartz veins are commonly formed and injected during mountain-building events at subsurface temperatures of 200–500°C and at depths exceeding 1km. Mountain building creates cracks in the rock, into which high-pressure, super-heated water is forced. At Marble Bar, as the water containing silicon, oxygen and iron cooled, the minerals precipitated to form jasper. Erosion has removed all the overlying material. And hey presto – Marble Bar in all its glory!

137. MATARANKA SPRINGS

Most visit Mataranka for its warm springs and its connection to early pastoral history through the ever-popular novel *We of the Never Never* by Jeannie Gunn. There are a number of springs that feed this, the headwaters of the Roper River.

Technically, these are not 'hot springs'. Hot springs are heated by columns of heat that have risen from deep down in the Earth to heat a section of the crust above. The water for Mataranka's two most popular springs – Rainbow and Bitter Springs – flow through limestone with the water in some cases coming more than 100km away before reaching the surface as the top of the water table. In its travels the water has

been 100m or more below the land surface. In most tropical areas, temperatures in the Earth's crust rise by 2.5°C per 100m with increases in depth. This is called the geothermal gradient. The average annual temperature at Mataranka is 28°C, so we expect water coming from more than 100m down to have temperatures in the low 30s. At Bitter Springs the water is an almost constant 34°C.

The quantity of water flowing from the springs is enormous; 300 litres per second at Bitter Springs (top) and around half that at Rainbow Springs. Although the total flow at Rainbow Springs (above right) is less, its flow is made more obvious by its smaller opening to the surface. Its water flow is best judged by the movement of water further away from its outlet.

Some sections of Bitter Springs are fed by seeps that are easily recognised by the swampy conditions along its banks. Bitter Springs may give off a gas that smells faintly of rotten eggs – this is hydrogen sulphide (H_2S). And its water has

a bitter taste (tasting is not recommended) from the presence of natural Epsom and other salts. But its water is crystal clear and deeper than at the more visited and touristy Rainbow Springs, which is nearer to town. At Bitter Springs one can swim or float downstream, then leave the water for a leisurely walk back along the riverbanks.

138. MENINDEE LAKES

Menindee Lakes are best described as 'augmented' nature. These lakes have been around for thousands of years and are part of the mechanism that is slowly filling the Murray–Darling Basin.

The Darling has flooded this region almost for ever, sometimes frequently but at other times only occasionally. Each flooding event leaves behind a coating of alluvium. Deposition, however, is uneven. It takes place most where the stream first slows; where it spills over its banks and onto the plain. This builds up natural levee banks that rise above the water as the river drains. The levees then act as barriers holding back water that forms backswamps. Furthermore, the river periodically takes new courses and/or abandons old ones. To these surface undulations are added sand and sandhills. It's not flat! So, following floods there have always been lakes. No trees grew at the centre of the deepest lakes as long periods of submergence would kill them.

The augmentation to these pre-existing lakes was the addition of infrastructure. Weirs were constructed to divert water into them and barriers and new channels formed to manage water flowing out of them (above right). Lake floodwater levels can be held for months and gradually released for irrigation or to initiate environmental flows.

Note that the more permanent enlarged lakes are ringed by dead trees. These trees once survived floods as they were not submerged for long enough periods to affect their drowning.

Darling River at Menindee.

Diversion Weir.

139. MIMOSA ROCKS

Mimosa Rocks is the end of a rhyolite lava flow. It was also the end for the paddle steamer *Mimosa* that ran aground nearby in 1863. Two lives were lost.

Rhyolite when erupted is viscous (thick, tacky and resistant to flow), but solidifies into sharp edged columns just like its sloshy sibling, basalt. Near-vertical columns of rhyolite are exposed on the island and adjacent headland. The true

colour of rhyolite is pale grey to fawn as exposed near the water level. The red colouring above this level is from the oxidisation of its low iron content. Rhyolite contains 70 per cent or more of quartz, giving it a chemical composition somewhat similar to that of granite, but it lacks granite's crystal structure due to its rapid cooling and solidification.

If you venture from the lookout platform onto the adjacent headland you will find the closely packed vertical columns of rhyolite (left) and washed-clean areas of exposed tops of columns that have not as yet weathered (below). The cracks are the result of shrinkage as the original lava flow cooled.

Between the lookout platform and Mimosa Rocks is a magnificent boulder beach consisting mainly of elongated smoothed-off rhyolite columns. Some boulders are up to 50cm long with the flat sides of the original columns still visible. As the island and headland are exposed to high-energy destructive waves and strong currents, the sand and finer gravels have been washed away.

140. MITCHELL FALLS

All waterfalls on the Kimberley are young. The Kimberley only
hauled itself above sea level around 200 million years ago. From
that point onward it developed a complete river system to drain the
new land. Erosion over the following 180 million years reduced the new Kimberley
to a featureless plain (opposite below). It was not until a fresh uplift 20 million
years ago that these waterfalls formed and began their march upstream. Such river
behaviour is termed rejuvenation and sparks a fresh cycle of erosion.

   Erosion is most rapid where streams run fastest, so it was along the new
north-facing escarpment that the freshly raised Kimberley was attacked. As
waterfalls erode they move upstream. The plunging water erodes deep pools at
the base of each fall by initiating shock waves that cause the submerged rock to
gradually disintegrate. Gravel and boulders washed down by the streams accelerate
this process. Parts of the cliff fall in and the falls move a little further upstream.
Over and over this process is repeated with cliffs falling and rocks disintegrating
and wearing away. Mitchell Falls have travelled upstream around 50km in the last
20 million years. The falls have cut through at least seven major strata (layers) of
horizontally bedded sandstone. Not only are the strata exposed in the falls, but also
on the dry ledges along the gorge's sides.

Photos: Carol Moore.

Upper Falls.

141. MOLONGOLO MEANDERS

Prior to the uplift of the Cullerin Range between the Lake George and Queanbeyan Faults (**#120**) commencing around 5 million years ago, the Molongolo River wandered across the gently undulating country between Captains Flat and Queanbeyan before being joined by the Queanbeyan River just downstream from the city. Uplift was slow and the Molongolo River was able to cut down through the ascending Cullerin Range at the same rate as the uplift. This created the Molongolo Gorge that runs from the Foxlow Basin in the east through to Queanbeyan on the Canberra Plain in the west. The range at this point is 8–10km wide, but the gorge is somewhat longer, as it and its river wind their way across the landscape. The wide, open gorge is approximately 100m deep.

One of the really interesting things about the gorge is that it tells us something about the river prior to the uplift – it was a much larger stream then than it is now.

How do we know that? Once the river started cutting down it became trapped within its old course no longer able to meander across its previous sections of flood plain. Not all the river's course had meanders, but there were a few. The easiest to view is from Sutton Road opposite the entrance to the Driver Training Centre (top). Now the thing about meanders is that they tend to have a diameter averaging around seven times the width of the stream. The river's width at the Sutton Road and others of its meanders is far, far less than one seventh the diameter of the meander. That's the evidence geologists use to support the statement that the river was once much larger. Meanders trapped within solid rock are said to be entrenched or incised.

Although entrenched, these meanders have many of the features of flood-plain meanders; a gentle slip-off slope on the inside of the bend and a steep, almost cliff, slope on the outside. The river's waters behave in a similar manner also. Water flows fastest on the outside of the meander and much slower on the inside. Erosion occurs on the outside and deposition on the inside.

Opposite: The gorge just upstream from the Sutton Road.

142. MONTGOMERY REEF

Unreal to spectacular, Montgomery Reef rises from the sea with
water pouring down its sides and fish scrambling to get off as
scavengers circle above to take advantage of an easy meal. All that
is true except for one word: 'rises'. It's an optical illusion. At sea and
away from the land, nobody notices tides. Here in north-western Kimberley, where
tides can exceed 10m, the emergence of Montgomery Reef occurs twice a day.

The Kimberley has Australia's best ria coast – these are coasts drowned by
rising sea levels. They are marked by sea cliffs, long thin peninsulas and sheltered
bays and inlets. The drownings took place during the last ice age stage from 2.5
million years ago to about 10,000 years before present. During this time sea levels
fluctuated from about 5m above those at present to 130m below. During the cold
periods Montgomery Reef was well away from the coast – a low sandstone plateau
and subject to common river-based erosion.

Montgomery Reef is not the usual tropical coral reef. It's classified as an
'inshore reef'. Inshore reefs lie close to the shore and isolated from other reefs.
This reef is large, approximately 350 square kilometres in size and 12km or more
away from solid land. The reef surrounds Yawajaba, a sandstone, mangrove-
covered Island. The reef is fragmented by numerous deep navigable channels.
At low tide much of the reef is only 5m above sea level, but at high tide, its surface
may be covered by as much as 5m of water. It is most spectacular on a falling tide
as water streams from its surface and down its steep edges.

There are no hard corals along the edges of the low tide exposed islands.
These corals cannot survive such exposure to the atmosphere (**#87**). Of prime
importance in the construction of the surface of Montgomery Reef are rhodoliths.
These are unattached, but often grouped, balls of calcareous algae that bounce
around on the reef's floor, often described as acting like tumbleweed. As water
drains from Montgomery on a falling tide, the rhodoliths collect and form boom-
gate barriers around the edges of internal lagoons. It is in these lagoons, where
water coverage is permanent, that hard corals survive and grow.

Montgomery Reef is in Camden Sound Marine Park – the most important
Humpback Whale nursery in the southern hemisphere. It is also home to turtles,
dugongs and numerous endangered fish and aquatic animals. Unfortunately it is
difficult and expensive to reach.

143. MOUNT ARAPILES

About 30 million years ago subsidence saw the Grampians area and the lower Murray inundated by the sea. Mount Arapiles (below) became an island – as it appears today, but in a sea of green. Later uplift saw this area restored to dry land.

Geologically, Arapiles is of interest because of its rock; it's quartzite. Quartzite is like an alternate form of granite. Granite commences as molten rock at or near the Earth's mantle. It crystallises as it cools and solidifies deep underground. Quartzite begins as sandstone sitting at or on the surface. Most sandstone is naturally cemented grains of broken down granite. Arapiles quartzite, when its sandstone parent was forced down in an ancient mountain building event, was compressed and heated to the point that it melted. Later it recrystallised, as it cooled and resolidified.

But there are differences between granite and quartzite. Granite contains feldspars – the mostly coloured bits that break down to clay – but these are not found in sandstone, and hence, not in quartzite. Also, cooling is faster in quartzite than in granite and quartzite's crystals are smaller and more tightly packed. The result is that quartzite is harder and more resistant than granite. When broken, quartzite breaks through its crystals rather than around their edges, as granite does.

Quartzite is relatively common in Australia and is the rock into which many of the MacDonnell Range gorges have been cut. The rock's qualities make Arapiles the most favoured abseiling site in the country.

'Mitre Rock' and 'Arapiles' climbing faces (below).

144. MOUNT AUGUSTUS

Mount Augustus's main claim to fame is its size. It's 8km long, 3km wide and rises 700m above the surrounding plain. If you search online for Mount Augustus you will find it generally described with added suffixes, such as the world's largest monolith, inselberg,

monadnock, and monocline, or just simply, rock. It's probably not the world's largest anything. I prefer to call it what it is. It's the eroded top of an anticline with rounded apex. The remainder of the anticline is buried beneath layers of sand and soil. It is asymmetrical in that slopes are steeper on the north-west-facing side of the anticline and gentler on the other.

The geology's relatively straightforward. Around 1.5 billion years ago, large rivers running across the region deposited huge quantities of sand and gravel on top of the already old and eroded granite. These deposits consolidated to form sandstones and conglomerates. Either sea levels rose or the land subsided, but the area then became a shallow seabed for more than 600 million years. Around 900 million years ago, strong north-east to south-west compression squeezed the land into its present anticlinal shape. Since then, erosion has had open slather. All the younger marine sediments have gone from the mount, plus much of the sandstone and conglomerate, even to the point of exposing the underlying granite (below left) at the north-west end of Mount Augustus in a location known as 'The Pound'. The term 'pound' is not used in the geologic sense as in Wilpena Pound, South Australia, but as in farming terminology. It really was used as a cattle pound.

Mount Augustus is difficult to get to. Perhaps that's to its advantage for those who want to see nature in a natural setting. And yes, it is twice the size of Uluru.

145. MOUNT BUFFALO

Mount Buffalo is Victoria's best example of granite; Wilsons
Prom (**#217**) is great, but Buffalo's even better. Mount Buffalo
is not really part of the Southern Alps; it's separated from them by faults and wide
valleys. Some would classify the plateau as a horst; an area surrounded by faults
and thrust upward during a period of uplift.

It didn't have surrounding faults and valleys when it formed. It was another
of those great granitic globs of magma (**#55**) that rose from
the mantle and into the lower crust around 400 million years
ago to help form the new and emerging south-east of the
Australian continent. The granite settled and cooled kilometres
below the surface, which had previously been a shallow
sea with underlying deep beds of shales, mudstones, tuff
(cemented volcanic ash) and limestones. This ancient seabed
was lifted above sea level by the rising granite. The intrusion
coincided with the great east-west squeeze that formed the
Lachlan Fold Belt (**#116**) and other fold systems in south-east Australia. It is hard
to visualise now, but at that time the weather on Mount Buffalo would have been
warm as its location is thought to have been not far north of the Equator.

In shape, Mount Buffalo is like a giant Uluru. It is solid granite from top to
bottom and from side to side. The sides are steep, and where slopes exceed 45°
there's nothing but bare rock. The plateau top is flattish with dotted tors and
rearing rocky outcrops.

It's well worth taking a closer look at the granite itself. It is coarser than normal;
probably because it cooled ultra-slowly allowing the crystals to grow over a longer
period of time than usual. Mount Buffalo's granite comes in a variety of colours
through orange and pink to grey. Some of the colour is embedded in the quartz
crystals, but most comes from the feldspars.

146. MOUNT ECCLES (BUDJ BIM)

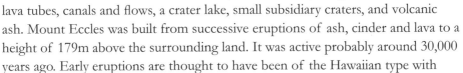

What I consider to be Australia's most complete volcano is
located 40km south of Hamilton. It has just about everything:
lava tubes, canals and flows, a crater lake, small subsidiary craters, and volcanic
ash. Mount Eccles was built from successive eruptions of ash, cinder and lava to a
height of 179m above the surrounding land. It was active probably around 30,000
years ago. Early eruptions are thought to have been of the Hawaiian type with
basalt lava flowing freely from lava lakes that filled
the three overlapping craters that are now occupied
by Lake Surprise. At various times it has spewed
forth dust, ash and cinder as well as lava. The cone
is composite, with thick layers of ash and scoria
covered by layers of varying thicknesses of lava.
Where the lava covering is thinnest, sections have
fallen away leaving scars on the sides of the cone.
Lava flows from Mount Eccles are probably the
longest in western Victoria with one reaching the
ocean near the town of Tyrendarra. Lake Surprise,
contained within Mount Eccles's triple crater, is
spring fed and has a maximum depth of only 14m.

Initially the lava flowed westward by canal out of the north-western end of the
lava-lake system and then southward through lava tubes. A blocked lava tube and

open canal system are still there at that
end of the lake, but beyond that point
requires some scrub bashing. However
there is a better alternative. Drive back
to just past the disused scoria quarry and
turn right to 'Natural Bridge'. Natural
Bridge is an intact section of a lava tube.
It's about 100m long and can be walked
through without the aid of a torch. Just
before the tube is a lava canal. The canal
(left) and tube (above) were part of a
short flow from some scoria cones that
developed just south of Lake Surprise
on the southern flank of Mount Eccles.

147. MOUNT KOSCIUSZKO GLACIATION

The Mount Kosciuszko Plateau of New South Wales is the only part of mainland Australia to experience glaciation within the Pleistocene epoch, roughly from 2.6 million years ago through to around 12,000 years before present. The epoch experienced four major cold periods and three interglacials. Some suggest that if in the near future we experience another glacial time, the past 12,000 or more years will also be considered interglacial. The coldest times are thought to have had temperatures as much as 9°C below present, but other periods were not quite so cold. Interglacials had temperatures similar to those today, with some slightly higher and others slightly lower. Quite wild

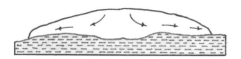

fluctuations in temperature between these extremes occurred within each glacial and interglacial period.

The last glacial maximum in Australia was around 20 million years ago, with rapid warming from 15,000 years ago through until the end of the epoch. It's difficult to establish many facts on the early glacial periods as evidence has been wiped out by subsequent glacial advances. Present-day surface evidence of glaciation at Mount Kosciuszko dates back to only the most recent major stage.

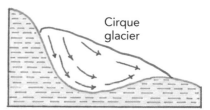

Cirque glacier

During that stage the Kosciuszko Region experienced two different types of glaciation. In the coldest of times, the whole landscape

You're not lonely at the top.

was smothered by a continental-type glacier. These glaciers move by extrusion. Weight at the deepest part of the glacier is sufficient to force out the edges. It's like the movement out from the centre of a pancake as it is being poured. This movement scrapes and rounds off the highest points. Note how smooth the Kosciuszko landscape looks.

In conditions a little warmer, but still cold, a different type of glacier forms. These are valley glaciers. Small glaciers form in the sheltered heads of valleys. These glaciers form cirques and slide downhill under the influence of gravity. The movement deepens valley floors giving them a distinctive U shape.

As a continent's highest mountain, Kosciuszko ranks last. It's not only last, but last by a long, long way. At 2,228m it is less than half the height of the next lowest of continental high points. It can be argued, however, that previously it was much higher and it is only Australia's extreme age that has allowed erosion to lower it to a stump of its former self.

Photo: Shutterstock | Greg Brave

148. MOUNT KOSCIUSZKO TRACKS

The ongoing commentary follows the Blue Lake Track from Charlotte Pass around to Hedley Tarn and Blue Lake, the Main Range Track to Carruthers Peak, Kosciuszko and Rawson Pass and the Summit Walk back to Charlotte Pass.

From Charlotte Pass the track drops steeply down to the Snowy River (left) that sits within a broad U-shaped glacial valley. From there on it's mainly uphill. A short offshoot return track leads to Hedley Tarn (below), which happens not to be a tarn at all. It's a morainal lake, blocked by an end moraine that marks the furthest extent of the glacier that scoured out Blue Lake. Tarn is a Scottish term for cirque, while an end moraine is a ridge of rocks, sand and soil that forms at the terminus of a glacier.

Blue Lake is a cirque lake. At various times when the Kosciuszko area was not totally covered by ice, snow accumulated on the southern side of Mount Twynam at this point, forming a small local glacier. The ice at the back of the glacier was deepest, causing the rear to slide down in a crescent-shaped motion scouring out both the back and the floor to form a cirque (**#147**). Blue Lake (opposite, top left) is 28m deep and covers 16 hectares.

Hedley Tarn.

The Blue Lake track joins the Main Range track near Carruthers Peak and follows along the top of the Great Dividing Range, first a little to one side and then over to the other, swapping all the way along. To the east lie the tributaries of the Snowy River, and to the west tributaries of the Swampy Plains River, a major feeder to the Murray.

The last lake, located on the western side of the divide, is Lake Albina (left). It's one of the prettiest lakes in the mountains and like Hedley Tarn is a morainal lake.

The Summit Walk section is a relatively easy as it follows the old road from Charlotte Pass to Rawson Pass, a distance of 8km, but it's not short of interesting glacial landforms such as some roche moutonees (#94) that have steep rocky ends and gently sloping tails. A great walk!

149. MOUNT LYELL

Queenstown's Mount Lyell is a great place to view and get a feel for rocks and landforms originating from the 500-million-year-old Mount Read Volcanics. Initial mining was for gold, but this proved to be unprofitable. Copper took over in 1893 and has been mined ever since. More than 1 million tonnes of copper, 750 tonnes of silver and 45 tonnes of gold have been produced, with a value in excess of 4 billion dollars in today's currency. Profits, however, came at a cost; pollution. Rehabilitation has been slow (opposite, top left).

One of Queenstown's now closed open-pit mines, 'Iron Blow' (below), is open to public view from a lookout just a few kilometres east of the town. It is signposted off the main highway to Derwent Bridge. An important fault, the Lyell Fault, is exposed in the pit and is visible in the image. It shows as a slightly curved, near vertical line, that runs up from the waterline to the top of the pit separating the yellow/brown Mount Lyell schists on the left from the pinky-purple Upper Owen Sandstone on the right.

A much closer look at the Lyell Schist can be had at the top side of the parking lot where you can get to touch it and inspect each streak of colour. The amazing gash exposed in the rock there is collateral damage from movement along the Lyell Fault long after the initial injection of lava and mineralised water 500 million years ago.

150. MOUNT SCHANK

It's thought to be 5,000 years old and related to the Mount Gambier volcanic complex (**#16**). From the road it appears to be a single volcanc but on closer inspection subsidiary craters can be identified on its flanks and in fields just north of the main crater.

Initial explosions were caused by rising magma contacting water within the

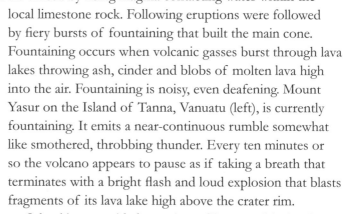

local limestone rock. Following eruptions were followed by fiery bursts of fountaining that built the main cone. Fountaining occurs when volcanic gasses burst through lava lakes throwing ash, cinder and blobs of molten lava high into the air. Fountaining is noisy, even deafening. Mount Yasur on the Island of Tanna, Vanuatu (left), is currently fountaining. It emits a near-continuous rumble somewhat like smothered, throbbing thunder. Every ten minutes or so the volcano appears to pause as if taking a breath that terminates with a bright flash and loud explosion that blasts fragments of its lava lake high above the crater rim.

Schank's steep-sided cone is readily accessible for those willing to climb the 333 steps to the top. Once there the view is incredible. Not just of the surrounding countryside but, of greater interest, the magnificent bowl-shaped crater. You really have to be keen to climb to the bottom of the crater as the floor reaches down to the level of the car park from where your climb started. There are no steps, just a rough track.

The car park lies on the merged flanks of a much smaller rocky cone and the dominant Mount Schank ash cone. The smaller cone is the original. It flowed basaltic lava onto the limestone plain where it is now quarried for road-building material.

151. MOUNT STURGEON AND MOUNT ABRUPT

Coming from the south of an evening, Mount Sturgeon and Mount Abrupt look like the upturned blade of a giant rip saw with one steep side and one gently sloping side. The Grampian Mountains, the south-western tail of the Great Dividing Range, was named by the great explorer Major Mitchell after mountains of the same name in his homeland, Scotland. Mitchell, a geologist, botanist and surveyor, was Surveyor General of New South Wales at the time. The shape of the two mountains gives rise to weather phenomena popularly called the 'Grampians Wave'. The wave develops in winds blowing from the west and is used by glider pilots to gain extreme altitudes.

Like the Grampians in Scotland, the Victorian Grampians have a complex geological history and have suffered their ups and downs in the past. During the past 450 million years they have experienced subsidence to

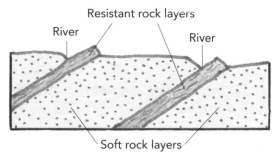

Resistant rock layers
River
River
Soft rock layers

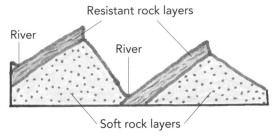

River — Resistant rock layers — River

Soft rock layers

beneath the sea, an intrusion of granite, uplift with intense folding and faulting, relentless erosion and further tilting and fracturing.

The main sandstone ranges of the Grampians have gentle

slopes to the west with steep rocky escarpments facing east. This type of landform is termed a cuesta. Cuestas form on inclined sedimentary rocks where rivers have been able to cut into softer strata, but upon striking a more resistant layer slide downhill by continuing to erode the softer layer. This leaves the more resistant layer to remain as a sloped capping.

When viewed from the north, the thickness of the resistant top stratum of Mount Abrupt is quite apparent (right).

Exposed outcrops of rounded granite boulders near Zumsteins and Halls Gap, and waterfalls on the Mackenzie River, provide added interest to the Grampian's landscape for visitors.

152. MOUNT WELLINGTON

This mountain of dolerite columns towers above Hobart's western suburbs. About 30 million years after the injection of dolerite (**#12**) much of Tasmania was buffeted by earthquakes as the supercontinent Gondwana

continued to fragment. Faults surrounding Mount Wellington and the whole range were pushed up by 500–600m. Like Ben Lomond (**#13**), Mount Wellington is a horst.

The top of Mount Wellington is quite varied. The western section slopes to the south and is covered by a battalion of vertical stone pillars 2–5m high. Just think of the joy it would have brought to the prehistoric English if something similar had been located close to Stonehenge. Most columns are standing upright, but a few have tilted to lean on their neighbours.

To the north-east (opposite page, top), the land is near flat, easy walking, dotted

with large boulders, and in spring and summer, covered by flowering shrubs.

Why the different surfaces? They were formed at the same time, the rocks are identical and the weather at both is indistinguishable. The difference is slope. Slope can and does affect the way in which weathering and erosion set about doing their work. On the steeper slopes water has washed the weathered material away. On the flatter summit, the tops of columns have weathered forming soil that has accumulated, allowing the growth of plants.

A magnificent example of a rock stream (**#168**) is located on the uphill side of the road, towards the summit. These boulders are the tops of dolerite columns that have weathered and fallen where they once stood. Any soil associated with the weathering has washed away and no plants grow. These rocks are stationary, they're going nowhere

153. MURPHYS HAYSTACKS

It's a great story. According to the information board, these are not haystacks, they're rocks. Apparently, a long time ago, an agricultural expert travelling in a horse-drawn coach noticed these rocks on the horizon and commented to fellow passengers that the farmer, Murphy, was a good farmer because he kept ample supplies of hay to feed his livestock in times of drought.

The information board also gives the true story – these rocks are inselbergs.

Inselbergs are isolated rocks of the granite family protruding from the ground. Some of the haystacks are sitting on their parent rock while others are floaters – they're sitting on sand between themselves and the solid rock beneath. And they're not all haystack shapes. Some resemble the Moai heads of Easter Island.

Originally, Murphys Haystacks were South Australia's version of the Devil's Marbles (**#56**). Then around 30,000 years ago, during the ice ages, the area was covered by wind-blown sand. If the Devils Marbles had been partly covered by sand at that time, they too might also look the same. At the end of the ice ages gradual erosion of the sandy soil around the haystacks began, exposing more and more of each haystack.

The largest of the Haystacks, and some others, have large caverns weathered into them. These caverns are examples of tafoni (**#178**), or, if your Italian is not up to scratch, cavernous weathering. The convex side of the haystack is protected by an impervious layer that stops salty water from seeping between the crystals that make up granite. This crust has been breached on the concave side, allowing water to enter the granite. As the water evaporates, salt crystals grow, forcing particles of sand from the surface. Continuous repetition of this process forms caverns.

Many haystacks remain as haystacks, but those attacked by tafoni have developed odd shapes.

154. MYRTLE BEACH

Now, if you want to take selfies in front of the line that marks
the transition from the underlying Lachlan Fold Belt (**#116**) to the
Sydney Sandstone Series, an example lies near the Murramarang
Resort on the south coast of New South Wales. Drive to the
resort, turn left (south) onto the gravel Old Coast Road, and carry on past the
Emily Miller Beach parking area. Turn left onto the signposted Dark Myrtle
Road and park at its end. The track to the left (north) leads to Dark Beach, the
one straight ahead (east) – the one you want – leads to Myrtle Beach. Walk 200–
300m along the track, turn right (south) on another well-used, but unsignposted
track that takes you down the steps to Myrtle Beach. Walk to the low cliffs at
the northern end of the beach, and there it is; the magical unconformity. The
author's hand is resting on the unconformity. The dark rock below the hand is of
Lachlan Fold Belt age while Sydney Basin rocks are above the hand. The line of
unconformity is somewhat wavy.

It's not only a place where two totally separate rock formations meet. It's where there is an age gap (unconformity) between the top of the bottom formation and the bottom of the top formation. That gap's around 100 million years. The top of the bottom formation lost hundreds, perhaps thousands of metres by erosion over a 100-million-year period before the Sydney Basin began to form on top of it.

Above the unconformity are patches of rock mish-mash (below). This is termed sedimentary breccia and may have been caused by landslides falling into a river feeding the accumulation of the Sydney Sandstone. The angular rocks in the breccia are mainly of Lachlan Fold origin glued together by sandstone.

Another unconformity here is nudist bathing – it's permitted on Myrtle Beach.

155. NARACOORTE CAVES

This is one of Australia's 'must-see' sites. For cave lovers it's probably not their best cave, but it's still good. But for those interested in Australia's original mega fauna, it's fantastic. This is a World Heritage site. For over 500,000 years the cave has been accumulating the bones of animals that simply fell in. They fell through the sinkholes that are scattered around the area (that are now fenced off to safeguard children).

Before entering the main display cave, Victoria Fossil Cave, spend some time at the nearby Wonambi Fossil and Information Centre. You have to go there to buy your cave tour tickets, so you may as well look around while you're there. The centre has extremely well-made life-like recreations of our ancient pre-human world. Or, as their information sheet states: "Stand face to face with megafauna and explore the depths of a cave and all the creatures within." To both kids and parents, it's fascinating.

Photo: Shutterstock | David_Chrastek

The cave was open to the public well before the discovery of its fossil bone chamber in 1969. Public admission also predates the current push for 'leave things just as nature left it'. Hence much of the floor is a discrete concrete path, and where thought necessary, the roof has been raised to accommodate taller members of the population.

You don't get to fiddle with the bones or to walk amongst them. You're left to kneel on a wooden platform and take your photos from 2m away, or just sit and gaze from deckchairs that overlook the scientific dig. Only a small section of the 50m by 20m by 4m-deep cave deposit has been exposed. There are more than 100 known fossil deposits at Naracoorte, but the one in the Victoria Fossil Cave is by far the largest.

Before making it to the fossils you pass through a variety of chambers with the usual speleothems. Many have brown tints, stained by tannin carried down from decomposing vegetation on the surface. Of special interest are the Helicities; the stalactites that grow whiskers (right). The prickly bits of helicities appear to defy gravity. No satisfactory explanation has been found, but growth by capillary action is possible. They are exquisite.

156. NARRYER GNEISS TERRANE

You won't find anything much if you go there, but you can at least say you've been there. The Narryer Gneiss Terrane contains what is thought to be the world's oldest pieces of rock. They're not just ordinary bits of rock, they're zircons. That's the gemstone you might have in an engagement ring if you can't afford diamonds. Zircons are crystals that form in most igneous rocks such as granite and basalt. They're generally small and of little value. The Narryer zircons are certainly small; you need a microscope to see them, but they're priceless.

And what of terranes? Well, they're important as far as the Earth is concerned. Terranes are pieces of the Earth's crust, the earliest of which existed before the continents as we know them came into existence. The first were formed by the lightest rocks floating to the surface on an ocean of molten magma where they solidified to form the proto crustal plates. Most of these rafts of solid rock floated around, occasionally bumping into one another and coalescing or breaking up. Eventually, most were recycled, but a few pieces survived. One such piece is the Narryer Gneiss Terrane exposed in the Jack Hills, which are part of Mount Narryer in Western Australia.

The Jack Hills gneiss, at somewhere between 3.3 billion and 3.8 billion years old is not the oldest rock in the world, but it contains minute zircons from an even earlier terrane that has long disappeared. These zircons are 4.2 billion to 4.3 billion years old, give or take the usual few years. When you consider that the Earth is 4.5 billion years old, these zircons are really, really old (#7).

And what is gneiss? Gneiss (opposite) is a type of rock, and in good English language fashion, it's pronounced 'niece'. In geological language it means a very resistant, ancient foliated metamorphosed rock. In ordinary language it means it's a special type of stripy hard rock. Metamorphic rocks are those that have been changed by the application of heat and/or pressure. For example, if shale is heated under pressure it changes to slate, if similar conditions are applied to limestone, the limestone will turn into marble, and even the humble sandstone changes to quartzite. If the heat and pressure are cranked up even further, these and other rocks can change again. Gneiss is one such rock. Rocks containing high quantities of silica (quartz), such as granite and quartzite, under extreme pressure remelt to a point where the crystal-forming process is reignited, forming a new crystalline rock called gneiss.

If you are in the area and like old things, you may well try for the Yarrabubba

Impact Crater. It's alongside the gravel road between Meekatharra and Sandstone. This crater is the oldest on Earth with an age of 2.2 billion years. Over that time, all the crater's outer debris circle has eroded away, but, surprisingly, the rebound impact point remains as a rocky hill that the road bends around. The hill, Barlangi Rock is even signposted. The original crater is thought to have been 70km wide.

157. NATIONAL ROCK GARDEN

An open-air museum of iconic Australian Rocks, this poorly
advertised gem is located near the banks of Lake Burley Griffin
and within sight of Parliament House. It would appear that one criteria for
selection and placement in the collection is size; nothing much less than around ten
tonnes makes the cut.

The National Rock Garden (NRG) was inaugurated in 2010 and given National
Monument status in 2011. You really need to know where it is. To find it, exit
from the Tuggeranong Parkway as if going to the National Arboretum, but instead
of turning uphill to the arboretum, turn towards the lake. A short road takes
you through a set of traffic lights and into the NRG. Each exhibit rock has an
information plaque attached. One face of the rock is usually polished, the others
are left natural. I visit about once a year to inspect new arrivals. Specimens include:
Pilbara iron ore (opposite, top); Moruya Tonalite, which is the granite used for
Sydney Harbour Bridge (opposite, bottom right); Tasmanian Dolerite; stacked
Bendigo Metasandstone; and Ballarat Quartz (opposite, bottom left).

The last pair mentioned are goldfields rocks. They are recent arrivals to replace
an earlier exhibit that contained flecks of gold that had been stolen.

Chinaman Creek Limestone.

158. NATURE'S WINDOW

Most people don't arrive in Kalbarri by accident. It's not on the main north road, nor is it close to a major city. Most come for sunshine, fishing, surfing and to ogle the wildflowers. But what do you do when the fish aren't biting, the surf's flat, it's cloudy and the flowers are out of season? You head to one or more of Kalbarri's permanent attractions such as Nature's Window.

Nature's Window is not far out of town and more than just a great place to photograph your favourite friend sitting in the window. It's also a window to nature. The hole has been caused by the rain and sand being blown against a narrow ridge, eroding a hole through the soft rock. Look closely at the rock; it's very different to its cousin, the massive, broad-banded Hawkesbury Sandstone that surrounds Sydney.

This sandstone was laid down during thousands of major flooding events in a shallow tidal sea somewhere between 400 million and 500 million years ago and

in most places exceeds 1km in thickness. Each flooding event is marked by thin stripes in the rock. The dominant red stripes indicate the presence of iron oxide in many of the flood deposits.

Also, look down at your feet. You are standing on ripple marks left in sand deposits that were

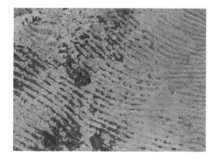

subsequently covered by other sand deposits from later flood events.

Then look at the view beyond the window; that's the Murchison River. It's the longest river system in Western Australia,

but well down the table in regard to annual water flow. Its headwaters are a series of salt lakes just north of Meekatharra. The horizon is generally flat with the river having cut a zigzag gorge into the plateau following major joint lines that developed during the region's uplift.

159. NINETY MILE BEACH

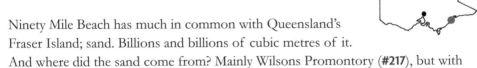

Ninety Mile Beach has much in common with Queensland's Fraser Island; sand. Billions and billions of cubic metres of it. And where did the sand come from? Mainly Wilsons Promontory (**#217**), but with some added from Mount Kosciuszko via the Snowy River.

The primary source of most sand is granite and other related crystalline rocks. When these rocks weather (decompose) they break down to their individual crystals of quartz, feldspars and mica. The feldspars become tiny clay particles that are removed by wind and waves and the small percentage of mica flakes are likewise removed or remain as glittering fragments within the sand. Sandstone can also be a substantial source of sand, but it too was once granite.

Wilsons Prom is quite a long way from Ninety Mile Beach – 270km by road – however, the distance is somewhat less if you follow the shore. But it's still a long way to haul all that sand.

If you look at a map you will notice not just one lake behind the beach, but a series of long narrow lakes that run parallel to the beach. Not that long ago, at the end of the last ice age 10,000–15,000 years ago, there were no Gippsland Lakes, just a Gippsland Gulf with the then non-existent towns of Sale and Bairnsdale having ocean frontage. Sand has been moved (**#84**)

from The Prom to close off the gulf and, at the same time, form Ninety Mile Beach and the Gippsland Lakes. Sand brought down to the coast by the Snowy River has provided additional sand for the eastern end of the region.

160. NORTH BROTHER

North Brother is one of three 'brothers' that are all closely related, as brothers generally are. North Brother is the most accessible, having a sealed road right to its very top. All are of similar age and formed of rocks with similar mineral content. The brothers are granodiorite, a rock that

contains a slightly lower percentage of silicon than granite and has cooled faster than granite but slower than rhyolite. The granodiorite is melted crust formed deep during subduction and brought back to near the surface where it has cooled at a slower speed than if it had been erupted onto the surface. Magma pushing

Above: Granodiorite looks like granite and erodes into blocks just like granite.

Below: Views from the top over Laurieton are panoramic.

up from below domed the surface, allowing the granodiorite to pool and solidify. Subsequent erosion has removed all the original surface together with the shattered original sedimentaries from the intrusion's flanks.

Coincidentally the name 'Three Brothers', given to them by Captain Cook, follows the same theme as used by the Aboriginal People whose Dreamtime stories have them as the burial places of three brothers killed by a spirit.

South Brother (far left) and Middle Brother (right, with TV mast). Photo taken from North Brother.

161. NULLARBOR PLAIN
THE ULTIMATE 'ARE WE THERE YET?' ROAD TRIP

For some people crossing the Nullarbor is fascinating; for others it's just plain boring. The land is treeless, not only because it receives little rain, but also because the rain that does fall sinks quickly into the underlying limestone rock and is carried away by underground drainage systems. The Nullarbor is the world's largest body of limestone (**#1**).

It dates back to the time of Australia's separation from Antarctica around 80 million years ago. As Australia drifted north, the crust between the separating continents stretched and thinned. The central southern part of the Australian Continent sagged, dipping gently towards Antarctica. By 50 million years ago the area now covered by the Nullarbor Plain lay under a shallow sea. It remained under the sea for the next 15 million years and during that time built up a thick layer of limestone from dead shellfish, bryozoans and algae. This rock, up to 300m thick, is called the Wilson Bluff Limestone and can only be seen at the foot of cliffs along the Great Australian Bight (**#25**). Much more of this stratum lies below sea level than above it.

This first limestone-building period ended with the onset of an ice age that saw sea levels fall dramatically and the emergence of the Nullarbor as a dry plain. From about 35 million years ago through to 10 million years ago the Earth went through several ice ages interspersed by warmer and drier conditions. Sea levels rose and fell and the Nullarbor oscillated between being dry land and ocean floor. During this period, two major deposits of limestone occurred. First the Abrakurrie Limestone Series, a dark brown layer up to 90m thick, and after that a thinner and younger layer referred to as the Nullarbor Series. It is the weathered Nullarbor Series limestone that now forms much of the surface of the plain.

Nullarbor in Latin means 'no trees', but only the central part of the plain is truly treeless. The surface is stony and partly covered by tufts of near-dead grass and hardy shrubs (above and below).

162. OCHRE PITS

Located close to the road between the Serpentine and Ormiston Gorges in the West MacDonnell Ranges are the Ochre Pits. The pits aren't your normal hole-in-the-ground type; they're in the cliffed bank of a small, normally dry, creek. The pits belong to the Western Arrernte people and its ochre is/was used by them for ceremonial body painting and also traded widely throughout central Australia. The ochre from here was considered superior

to most and had a wide colour range from white to yellow, brown and red. Please don't take samples.

Ochre is fine silt and clay stained by iron and other oxides. These thin layers of varying colours started life as flat layers of silt and mud at the bottom of a shallow ocean. That was around 800 million years ago. Over the next 400 million to 500 million years these deposits grew to be up to 10km thick in some places. The sediment's own weight compressed the silt and mud into rock. Between 340 million to 300 million years ago all this was squeezed, forming the folded MacDonnell Range and forcing the once-horizontal ochre strata into near-vertical positions.

The white colour is clay containing aluminium oxide – commonly called kaolin or china clay. The red is slightly coarser and includes iron oxide (rust), while the yellow is a clay with muted amounts of the same oxides.

163. ORGAN PIPES

Gawler Ranges' Organ Pipes are so very different to their namesake which lies outside Melbourne (**#111**). The processes involved in their forming were the same, but nothing much else.

The Gawler Craton is one of Australia's three main building blocks (**#7**), having been in place for around 2.7 billion years. The craton continued to build for around a further billion years to reach its ultimate size. In that 1 billion years it experienced numerous granite intrusions, very aggressive erosion and, importantly, several floods of lava. Lava squeezed up between the granites, flowed over the top of them and eventually welding the lot together.

Much of the lava was rhyolite, which is usually thick and tacky when erupted, but in the Gawler Ranges it flowed easily due to the presence of fluorine gas which altered the lava into a free-flowing liquid. As the lava cooled and solidified it shrank, creating tightly packed four-, five- and six-sided columns (**#33**).

At the Organ Pipes site an ancient but still functioning stream has cut a valley into the rhyolite, exposing its vertical columns. On the gentler slopes above the cliffs, columns can be seen leaning into the valley waiting to fall. The red/pink colouring of the columns is caused by the presence of iron in the rhyolite.

The Gawler Ranges lie north of the Eyre Highway, but as the area is sparsely settled all access roads are gravel. The Organ Pipes lie just inside the Gawler Ranges National Park to the north of Minnipa. The last few kilometres of the access road passes through private land and is poorly maintained. Four-wheel drive or all-wheel drive vehicles are strongly recommended.

164. PARLIAMENT HOUSE ROCKS

The Canberra Region has some of the most fascinating and easily viewed geology in Australia. Both the old and new parliament buildings sit above road cuttings that expose the region's underlying geology.

Unfortunately, State Circle has no parking; so best head along Kings Avenue, cross State Circle and find parking near the 'new' parliament house. Walk down as if to take the photograph (opposite, above).

About 500 million years ago Australia was firmly attached to Antarctica, but Australia was smaller and not even near where it is today. Canberra lay under the ocean off the coast and, according to some scientists, north of the Equator. Coral grew around some ancient volcanic islands and shellfish inhabited the warm shallow waters. Mud, sand and silt were washed into the ocean to eventually become mudstone, sandstone and shale.

Starting about 450 million years ago and lasting for about 100 million years Canberra became part of the big squeeze that formed the Lachlan Fold Belt (**#116**). This large region of extreme compression saw solid rock layers concertinaed into folds and the formation of long fractures and faults along which rock strata slid

Road cutting, 'old' Parliament House.

against each other. Most of these folds and fault lines run close to north-south in direction and can still be seen in the lie of the present-day landscape.

Exposed on State Circle are some fabulous examples of folds, faults and unconformities resulting from the big squeeze (**#116**). In the photos, note that sandstone (dark brown) at the top of the road cutting has been pushed over the much-folded State Circle shales (pale brown) that lie below them. The sequence of deposition of oldest at the bottom and youngest at the top has been maintained, but there is an age gap of millions of years between the top of the folded shale layers and the bottom of sandstone layers. Such a gap is referred to as an unconformity (**#106** and **#154**).

165. PHILLIP ISLAND ROTTING ROCKS

These rocks aren't smelly; but they are rotting. They're to be found at the popular Woolamai Beach on Phillip Island. Just walk along the beach until you reach an outcrop of colourful rocks that are located 20m past the stairs that lead from the beach to the start of the Cape Woolamai walking track. These rocks are saprolite.

About 50 million years ago this was a basalt lava flow. The basalt with its solid rock columns has been transformed and replaced by some of its own minerals. The name saprolite comes from the Greek language and roughly translates to 'rotten rocks'. The basalt has literally rotted away. This rotting is normally referred to as chemical weathering. The weathering commences at the edges of columns. The gaps between columns are widened by the chemical reaction between water, air, and the basalt. Basalt contains more than 60 per cent feldspars that break down to form clay. The phosphates, silica, iron, aluminium and other minerals are then removed by erosion and/or further chemical reactions. These processes have gone on for millions of years until little original basalt remains.

Ground water on Phillip Island is mildly acidic, a feature that accelerates the disintegrating processes. The iron oxides mainly accumulated at the edges of the basalt columns leaving the leached white clay as the dominant component of saprolite. Aluminium compounds may add a yellow or orange colouring. The example of saprolite (below right) lies closer to the sea than the others (below left and opposite). Wave action has removed the softer saprolite, exposing some more resistant samples that still contain solid basalt cores that are yet to rot away

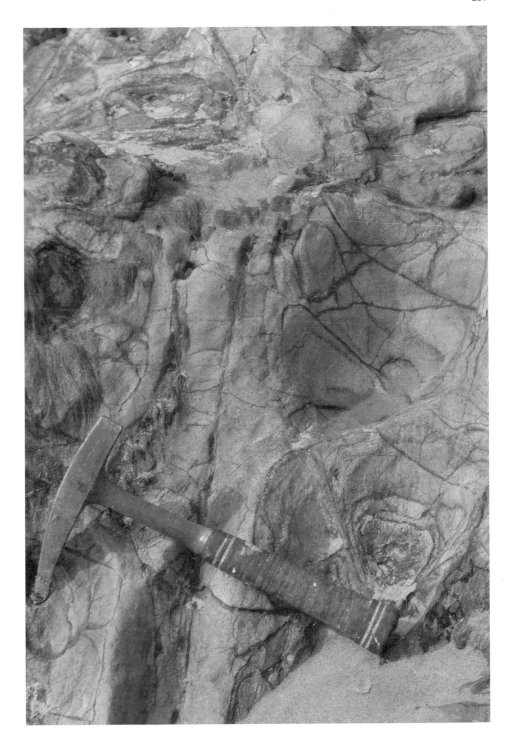

166. PILBARA HEMATITE

Iron ore is one of Australia's most profitable exports and huge quantities of it exist in the Pilbara. Hematite (Fe_2O_3) is an oxide of iron and chemically much the same as common rust ($Fe_2O_3.nH_2O$). Take away the H_2O (water) part and we have hematite. Hematite, however, is not quite perfect iron oxide; it contains impurities. It's the impurities that separate one iron ore from another. Pilbara's ore is up to 66 per cent pure iron.

The sedimentary rocks that now form the Hamersley Ranges commenced accumulating in an ocean basin more than 3 billion years ago. These sedimentaries formed at a time when oxygen levels were extremely low, and life on Earth as we know it had not yet evolved.

Around 2,750 million years ago the Earth's land surfaces consisted of iron-rich bare rock, sand and dust; no soil, no trees, no swamps, no grass and no animals. The oceans were salty, had a high dissolved iron content and contained no fish. Earth then entered a period of change. For the next 1 billion years the world's seas periodically hosted masses of a newly evolved form of cyanobacteria (commonly referred to as blue-green algae). Each bacteria-rich period lasted for millions of years. In a simple chemical reaction the bacteria used sunlight to photosynthesise, splitting water into its components of hydrogen and oxygen. It is thought that some of the oxygen then joined with the dissolved iron to precipitate as iron oxide and fall to the ocean floor. The remaining oxygen and hydrogen eventually made its way into the atmosphere.

Once the ocean's dissolved iron was used up, the process came to a halt, but sedimentation continued, building a non-iron layer on top of the iron oxide layer. Over time the ocean's dissolved iron content gradually regrew. The cyanobacteria again flourished and the whole process was repeated over and over building up alternating bands of iron-rich and iron-poor sediments termed Banded Iron Formations (BIFs). Over 1 billion years the BIFs became kilometres thick, and most importantly, the oxygen in the atmosphere rose to a point where it could support oxygen-using organisms. BIFs are found in all continents, it's just that Australia has more than most. The layering of BIFs in the Pilbara was terminated by uplift 2,200 million years ago.

Photo below: Shutterstock | Ryan Hoi

Photos above: Chris and Judy Pratt.

167. PILLIGA SANDSTONE CAVES

The Pilliga is an ill-defined area in north-central New South Wales, mainly recognised by its vegetation. Underlying much of the mixed cypress/eucalypt scrub is sandstone; Pilliga Sandstone. The sandstone was laid down on the bottom of long gone freshwater lakes that existed there around 150 million years ago. In places the sandstone is up to 300m thick. The caves of interest are located off the Newell Highway between Coonabarabran and Narrabri. As these caves are on Aboriginal land it's best to seek directions and advice at the Pilliga Forest Discovery Centre in Baradine before going there.

Most of these caves are the result of a process termed cavernous weathering. Cavernous weathering is driven by salt and the resulting landforms are termed Tafoni (**#178**). Back-to-back tafoni caverns have resulted in the formations of arches and tunnels. The lowest exposed stratum on this plateau peninsula is very poorly cemented and care should be taken not to degrade the surface.

Of particularly interest is an archaeological site (below right). It contains grooves worn in the sandstone by early Gamilaraay people sharpening axes and other stone implements. The grooves are clearly visible from behind a protective grill. The ledge of white sandstone into which the grooves have been worn is at a comfortable working height above the cave floor.

The track along the plateau peninsula features art works that acknowledges the original aboriginal culture of the Pilliga.

168. PINE LAKE BLOCK STREAMS

Pine Lake is written up in the *60 Great Short Walks* pamphlet available at most Tasmanian information centres. The walk is short; just 400m long, and elevated half a metre above the ground. Halfway along the boardwalk you will cross an odd-looking feature – a block-stream. These are sometimes referred to as block fields. With both these names, 'block' may be replaced by 'rock' just to confuse. I prefer to use the term 'block stream' for formations such as this narrow one at Pine Lake. Block field may be more appropriate where the collection of rocks is much broader, as at Ben Lomond (**#13**).

Block streams or block fields should not be confused with 'talus' or 'scree' as these terms are used to describe piles of rock at the foot of a cliff or steep slope where the rocks have reached their position by falling from above. Block streams are formed in situ, that is they have not moved from anywhere. The stream at

Pine Lake was once solid dolerite rock that has disintegrated into a pile of rocks by frost wedging. Underneath this jumble of rocks is the same (but solid) rock waiting to do the same thing. Dolerite has a multitude of vertical and horizontal cracks, and under the right weather conditions is prone to frost wedging. Water seeps into cracks, and when temperatures fall below 0°C it freezes and expands. As temperatures rise the water thaws, but in the meantime grains of sand have moved into the cracks stopping the rocks from returning to their exact former positions. Block streams have slopes of around 25° or less.

Rock streams are classified as being periglacial. When used as a prefix, 'peri' means near or around. So periglacial features are found near glaciers. They are relatively common in Tasmania at altitudes between 700–1,000m.

Boardwalk and fog at Pine Lake.

169. PINNACLES (NSW)

The colours are brilliant; a rich red top layer dribbling over a stark white lower layer. Viewers are almost overwhelmed by the contrast of colour. The dribbles are surface features only. They

come from fragments of the top layer having fallen or been washed down from the red strata above. The red layer is a gravelly clay containing an abnormally high iron content, while the white layer is sandy.

It is thought that these layers developed 25 million to 30 million years ago under much warmer conditions than presently exist, and well away from the sea. The sharp line that separates the two colours marks the water table (**#77**) that

Photo: Shutterstock | Alf Manciagli

existed at that time. Above that line the formation has been laterised. (A process common in seasonally wet-dry tropical regions where iron in base rocks is dissolved and moved towards the surface by capillary action leaving the bottom layer free of iron.)

The Pinnacles are named for the sandy towers developed at the foot of the cliffs where a small seasonal stream has cut its gully. Access to the gully floor is difficult. The Pinnacles are viewed from a well-made circular track that starts and finishes at its car park, which is signposted off the Princes Highway south of Pambula.

170. PINNACLES (NAMBUNG NP)

It's hard to imagine any other natural formation that looks even remotely like the Pinnacles; they are exposed limestone mini-towers. The towers vary in size. Most are from 1–4m high and 1–2m wide.

The geology of this section of the coast is quite recent, with the exposed Pinnacles built during and after the last ice ages. Over the last 2 million years there have been four major and numerous minor glacial stages that have caused wide fluctuations in sea level. During falling sea levels, vast areas of sand were exposed and opened to transportation inland by the onshore westerly winds that still blow in the area. Later, as temperatures warmed and sea levels rose, constructive waves pushed sand up the beach, piling up more and more sand for eventual removal inland by the wind. As each glacial/interglacial cycle was repeated, the volume of sand increased to build a wide dune system stretching kilometres inland from the coast. As the sand's origin was the seabed, it contained vast quantities of shells that were broken and smashed as they were blown inland. The last cold period climaxed between 60,000 and 20,000 years ago. The cold periods were accompanied by higher rainfall along the Western Australian coast. Acidic water percolating through the sand dissolved the calcium carbonate in the seashells and carried it down to lower levels where it precipitated, cementing the sands into a weak grainy limestone termed calcarenite.

At the time that the limestone was forming in the lower layers, the upper layer was developing soil on which native vegetation grew. It is thought that tree roots played a role in breaking up the limestone before the vegetation died and the topsoil blew away exposing the sand and broken calcarenite.

171. PORONGURUP RANGE

It is believed that the Porongurup Range formed around 1,200 million years ago with the initial collision of Australia and Antarctica. The collision occurred at the same time as a large injection of granite occurred in the south-west of Western Australia. The timely arrival of this granite welded the two continents together. The bumping together of the two weakened the crust under that part of Australia and allowed the granite to intrude higher into the crust at the site of the Porongurup Mountains. Over more than a billion years, the older rock above the granite and the upper levels of the granite have eroded away leaving a series of remnant granite domes forming a range that is now only 15km long.

It's a bit of a climb, but one of the most rewarding walks is from the Castle Rock car park to the Granite Skywalk (above and below right) and return; allow at least two hours. The ultimate goal is reached by climbing a ladder and then traversing the vertigo inducing Skywalk that encircles part of the top. The granite boulders surrounded by and near the Skywalk are massive; and very, very old.

The Stirling Ranges, only 30km north of the Porongurups, were formed by the break-up of the same two continents as the supercontinent Gondwana fragmented.

Photos: Ian Boxall.

172. PRINCESS MARGARET ROSE CAVE

The cave is notable for its colour, stalactites and columns, and
for having an unusually flat floor. The cave developed in young
limestone around 800,000 years ago. At that time the Glenelg River had not cut
down to its current position, but sat at a level approximately 15m higher than
now. Slightly acidic water seeping down a minor fault line that intersected the
river formed caves at the level of the river. As the river gradually lowered its bed,
the floor level of the cave fell with it. This explains two factors of the cave's
geography; its flat floor and almost straight alignment. As the Glenelg River eroded
and lowered its bed over time, it left the cave high and dry.

The line of fault in the cave's ceiling
is marked by a row of stalactites (below
left). White sections of the cave's roof
and walls are the exposed parts of the
original caves as dissolved by water.
The pale coloured sections have been
formed or covered by limestone crystal
(calcite) that has precipitated from
surface water draining down through
the roof's fault line. The brown colour
is tannin stain. Tannin is a weak acid formed from decaying vegetation and is the
same liquid that gives forest streams their brown colour (#1).

173. PURNULULU'S BEEHIVES (BUNGLE BUNGLES)

You need a four-wheel drive, a plane or a helicopter to get into the Bungle Bungles, but once you get there the rock formations will astound you. Gigantic striped beehive domes stand to attention like China's entombed warriors over an area of hundreds of square kilometres. Their existence has only became widely known in the last 30 years.

The rocks of the Bungle Bungles had their beginnings around 375 million to 350 million years ago. Streams flowing from the Osmond Range in the north, and long since eroded ranges near Halls Creek in the west, washed huge quantities of sand and gravel into the upper reaches of the Ord Basin. Unlike much of the sandstone in other parts of Australia, the Bungle Bungle sandstone evolved on dry land. Sandstones laid down on dry land are comparatively weak when compared with those developed on the seabed, as the latter generally contain calcium derived from shells and fish skeletons. This calcium forms a type of cement that binds the sand grains together.

The true colour of the Bungle Bungle Sandstone is almost white, a reflection of its high quartz content. The surface, however, is marked by near-horizontal alternating bands of orange and black. The colours are caused by differences in clay content in the alternating rock strata. A veneer of algae that grows on the clay-free strata forms the black bands. Water can percolate through these layers keeping the algae alive during the dry season. Orange strata surfaces indicate the presence of clay. These strata become so dry in the April to November season that algae cannot survive. The orange colour is a surface staining of iron and manganese oxides.

Photos: Carol Moore.

174. QUARRY BEACH

Quarry Beach at Mallacoota could have been more appropriately named 'Rainbow Beach', but that wasn't to be. The rocks here are amongst the most colourful I have ever seen. They are the southern end of the Narooma Accretionary Complex (**#42**); one of those strips of old seafloor attached to Australia over 400 million years ago.

As a spreading proto-Pacific Ocean subducted below the Australian Plate it scraped off some of its seafloor onto the growing south-east coast of Australia. This was all part of the Lachlan Fold System referred to elsewhere in this book (**#116**). The rocks include various cherts (related to flint), slate and other metamorphosed sedimentary rocks. These rocks were initially carried down by the subduction and placed under great heat and pressure, but were then squeezed back towards the surface.

Exposure at Quarry Beach has been assisted by pounding from high-energy ocean waves and the quarrying of the rock for construction purposes.

175. RAINBOW BEACH

If you want the town, put 'Rainbow Beach' into the navigator; if you want the beach, add 'Rainbow Beach Road' and drive to its end; park, head south and take care. The beach is backed by steep sand cliffs. Not the place to be trapped if the waves are up and the tide's

coming in. The best time to walk the beach is from about two hours after high tide until low tide.

The cliff-face colouring comes from the presence of minerals such as iron oxide, rutile, ilmenite and monazite and the accumulation of humus. The iron provides the reds, browns and yellows, while the humus is responsible for most of the blacks and greys. Leaching removes some chemical colours from some places and causes it to accumulate in others. The splotches of white are simply fresh sand blown up from the beach or sand that has been blown from the young dunes that lie sheltered behind the older coloured dunes (#37). The ancient dunes have been sculpted by surface run-off from the hard-packed sand into a stunning range of pinnacles and contorted shapes.

The northern end of the cliffs is marked by the presence of coffee rock. Coffee rock, up close, has the same colour as proprietary brands of dark chocolate rather than the colour of coffee, but they say it turns water a coffee colour during storms. The rock is smoothish with no jagged edges and is related to lignite (brown coal, #123). Coffee rock is a sedimentary rock and is exposed here and in like places such as Fraser Island and on Maroochydore Beach. Coffee rock in these areas is thought to have initially formed as floors to the bottoms of perched lakes (#77) during lower sea level periods in the recent ice ages. It is a mixture of decayed and partly decayed humus together with sand and clay. Careful inspection will reveal fragments of branches, charcoal and leaves. The presence of coffee rock is seen as a protector of beaches and sand hills.

The flat hard sand at the foot of the cliffs is used at low tide by four-wheel-drivers as a highway between Rainbow Beach and Double Point Headland.

Photo: Shutterstock | Chris Andrews Fern Bay

176. RAINBOW VALLEY

Rainbow Valley is more the remains of a crumbling plateau's peninsula than a valley. No matter what, it's spectacular. If photography your interest, you're in luck; the cliffs face south-west with the sun on them most of the day.

The geology is quite straightforward. The surface here is old, a remnant of the ancient James Ranges that had been gently folded hundreds of millions of years earlier. Erosion has cut the surface into a series of gently sloping flat-topped mesas with deposition filling the area between the mesas with the eroded sand. As you drive into the park the colourful south-west-facing cliffs grab your attention. The cliffs have formed on the side of a ridge that juts out from a small mesa that in the photo (opposite, above) hides behind the left half of the cliffs.

Photo: Shutterstock | Marc Witte

To the left of the rock face, and contrasting with it, is flat land and a small intermittent lake. These features emphasise the landscape's age. Eroded material has smothered the prior landscape leaving Rainbow Valley's plateau standing proud.

Following the separation of Australia from Antarctica, Australia has drifted northwards and become progressively hotter and drier. Rain falling in wet periods percolated into the sandstone and dissolved most of the iron and some silica. In dry periods the water carrying its dissolved load rose to the surface where it evaporated, leaving its load behind to accumulate in the upper layers. The 'cemented' upper layer is much more resistant to erosion, but the soft and poorly compacted sandstone has undercut the resistant layer in the centre of the cliffs. The sandstone is now rapidly (in geological terms) eroding away.

The true colour of the sandstone is white as can be seen in the photo (above) of a section of cliff face that has recently fallen away. The sand that continually weathers from the cliff faces is also white.

177. RED ROCK

From 2 million years ago and until recent times, great swathes of central Victoria were periodically covered by fresh lava and volcanic debris from numerous volcanic outlets.

Red Rock, 5km west then 10km north of Colac, is one such outlet; it's a group of maars (**#198**). Volcanic activity here occurred between 12,000 and 7,000 years ago. The twin craters may have flowed some lava in their early life, but what you see now is material ejected by explosive younger eruptions. This material includes older blocks of basalt, some limestone that underlies the area, and huge quantities of scoria and volcanic ash.

During really energetic eruptions large blocks of solid rock were thrown into the air. Basalt blocks weighing up to one tonne can be found near the top of Red Rock Volcano. A disused quarry on the side of Red Rock and adjacent to the picnic area is an excellent place to look for blocks, scoria and ash.

The Red Rock scoria (below), like most scoria, is riddled with holes and looks like mini honeycomb. Those holes are from escaped gas. Many of the droplets of molten lava flung into the air during fountaining are blasted apart by this escaping gas to form the smaller particles of ash and dust.

The two lakes immediately below the lookout have the classic form of maars. That is, they have steep inward-facing slopes and gentler outward-facing slopes. They were formed when rising magma contacted water in the overlying limestone, heated the water to a point where it turned to steam, and in separate gigantic explosions blasted out the rock above forming the wide shallow craters. Colour in the lakes is from algal growth.

The lake in the background of the photo (opposite) is Lake Corangamite, Australia's largest permanent saltwater lake. It was formed by lava flows damming several small local streams.

178. REMARKABLE ROCKS

Yes, they are remarkable. They just happen to be the right rocks, in the right location, at the right time. The rocks are granite sitting on top of their parent, a granite dome. They are the remnant surface of the dome which was once larger. The upper surface had broken into large cubes as it expanded after the overlying rock had been eroded away (**#55**). The present dome has horizontal and vertical cracks running through it but these cracks are extremely fine not permitting the inflow of water or air. Most of the top layer of cubes that were separated by wider cracks has weathered away and those remaining are fast going the same way.

The individual rocks are being attacked by cavernous weathering. Technically known as tafoni, such caverns develop in some exposed granites in both coastal and arid locations. These locations have one thing in common, the presence of salt. Water containing salt seeps into the miniscule gaps between the rock's crystals. When the water evaporates, the salt crystallises forcing the rock particles further and further apart each time the wetting and drying sequence is repeated. Loose grains of sand fall off allowing the salty water to penetrate deeper into the granite. The caverns may have diameters and depths ranging from several centimetres to well over two metres. Cavernous weathering only affects those surfaces that water can penetrate. Once underway the caverns so produced keep growing, even to the point of coalescing one with another.

If you look closely at Remarkable Rocks granite you will notice imbedded in it some large foreign-looking stones that are obviously not granite. These are

xenoliths (zen-o-liths), from the Greek meaning 'foreign stone'. Xenoliths have a higher melting point than granite and so hold their identity when surrounded by the granite as it rises from deep down and melt their way into the lower crust before solidifying.

179. RIVERSLEIGH FOSSILS

Riversleigh fossil beds lie 50km south of Lawn Hill (**#124**). Considered to be one of the three most important fossil beds in the world, they contain specimens spanning the most recent 25 million years of Australia's biological and geological history. The beds contain fossils of giant snakes, marsupial lions, carnivorous kangaroos and hundreds of other weird and wonderful animals. They can be a viewed as

a DIY expedition or on a guided tour. There are a number of information boards at the site to provide facts, but the presence of a knowledgeable guide makes the experience all the more rewarding.

Site D is the only part of the World Heritage-listed area open for casual inspection. This site is located on the top of a ridge accessed by a short and steepish but well-made track. The young limestone at the top that contains the fossils is about 24 million years old and rests on slightly older conglomerate. The conglomerate formed the bed of a lake into which a large river flowed. We know this from the coarseness of the stones that comprise the conglomerate. The orange-grey and sometimes pebbly limestone contains the fossils.

The fossils include 'Big Bird' (below), which is a *Dromornithid*, and a crocodile jaw (opposite, below).

180. RONNY CREEK GLACIAL DEPOSITS

There are few places in Australia where you can view samples of glacial erosion, but there are even fewer places that you can visit to see relatively uneroded examples of glacial deposition. Ronny Creek, towards the southern end of the Cradle Mountain access road, is one such place. For a short period of time the retreating Cradle Mountain collection of glaciers (**#50 and 61**) ended here and deposited their loads. At that time the depth of moraine may well have exceeded 50m.

On both sides and further along the road towards Dove Lake are some well-defined and less controversial moraines. These moraines are groups of low ridges, with some aligned north-south and others more east-west. The moraines' upper surfaces are covered by angular blocks of rock, low shrubs and button grass. They are well above the poorly drained area of Ronny Creek and mark the approximate high surface point for one or more of the glaciers. All these smaller glaciers melted by the end of the age around 10,000–12,000 years ago.

Back to Ronny Creek... Just upstream from the bridge is a group of one large and a number of smaller shallow lakes. These lakes are 'kettles' and the humps around them are 'kames'. Why the names? I don't know. Kettles form in holes left by the slow melting of buried blocks of ice. During glacial retreat, rivers form on and under the ice. If this occurs upstream from the snout, sections of the glacier can become separated from the main body of ice. As the bottom of a glacier lies well below the level of its end moraine, continued melting will cause the surface of the isolated sections to melt faster than their buried sections. At some point the surface of the ice section blocks and that

of the moraine will become level. Continued melting of the upstream glacier will wash down sand, gravel and rocks to cover the isolated blocks. When the blocks eventually melt, kettle holes remain and may fill with water.

181. ST. COLUMBA FALLS

St Columba is reputed to be the tallest waterfall in Tasmania.
Saint Columba Falls stagger over the edge of rough, occasionally
near-vertical cliffs, splitting into more and more sections as the
water descends. They're pretty and much higher than they appear to be in the
photograph. They drop 90m from a catchment that drains the south-eastern side
of Mount Albert. The large catchment area guarantees a continuous flow all year
round. These falls are categorised as 'horsetails'.

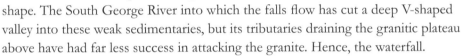

   The rock behind the fall is the same granite as seen
along the nearby east coast (**#11 and 14**), but the rocks
out from the base are much older. These are softer,
slightly metamorphosed shales and siltstones. Nearly
400 million years ago the granite rose from below and
intruded the sedimentaries. It partly cooked the shales
and sandstones and in places compressed them out of
shape. The South George River into which the falls flow has cut a deep V-shaped
valley into these weak sedimentaries, but its tributaries draining the granitic plateau
above have had far less success in attacking the granite. Hence, the waterfall.

   The well-made but steepish track down to the falls is through cool-temperate
rainforest lined with ferns of all sizes and young trees. The valley floor is dotted
with rounded granite boulders and magnificent groves of Dicksonia Tree Ferns.

   St Columba Falls can be reached from either Pyengana or Ringarooma along
well-made gravel roads.

182. SAWN ROCKS

Sawn Rocks formed in a lava flow from Mount Kaputar, but is accessed by a different road; the Narrabri to Bingara highway. It is one of the most spectacular rock sites in New South Wales; a

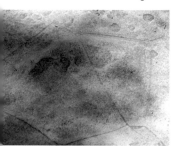

magnificent example of columnar development by cooling in volcanic rock. As lava cools and solidifies it contracts in size. This leads to the development of fine cracks that extend from the surface through the cooling lava to eventually reach the bottom of the flow (**#33**). As lava flows can be hundreds of metres thick the cooling, solidifying and cracking processes can take many years.

Sawn Rocks is very accessible with a wheelchair-friendly path from its parking area to a viewing platform. Furthermore, you don't need to be an abseiler to get a hands-on, close-up view. Some intact clusters have fallen to the ground as a result of undercutting by the creek at the foot of the cliff. This same stream also exposes the tops of columns along its worn bed verifying the conclusion that the original lava flow was even thicker than the height of the cliffs.

The columns are so closely packed, it is impossible to poke a knife blade between them.

183. SHARK BAY STROMATOLITES

Shark Bay could best be described as an oceanic backwater. Due
to the sandy nature of the surrounding land and low annual
precipitation, no freshwater streams of any consequence enter the
bay to flush it out. Barrier islands also partly block the bay's entrance
thus inhibiting the tidal flow of water in and out. Much of the water within the bay
remains within its confines for months or even years. Evaporation from the surface
is quite high and results in the water becoming extremely salty. Water in Hamelin
Pool at the southern end of the bay is twice as salty as normal seawater.

It is in this saline environment that we find stromatolites. To the eye,
stromatolites look like large concrete cauliflower heads growing in the shallow
waters at the edge of a bay. Stromatolites grow under these conditions, not because
they require salt, but because the high salt content and the lack of nutrients in the
water preclude the growth of competing organisms.

Stromatolites were among the first living organisms on Earth and date back at
least 3,500 million years; that's more than three-quarters of Earth's history. Not

that the stromatolites at Hamelin Pool are of this age. They have only developed here since the end of the last ice age. Each stromatolite contains millions of microscopic cyanobacteria (blue-green algae) as a community arranged as a thin veneer over its rocky surface. The algae trap very fine particles of sediment in mucus they secrete. The algae also extract calcium carbonate from the seawater so that when the algae die the sediment, mucus and calcium carbonate form natural cement. The stromatolites at Hamelin Pool grow at a rate of 0.3–0.5mm annually, so those in deeper water, about 1m high, are more than 1,000 years old.

A live specimen is kept under controlled conditions in a glass tank at the nearby historic Hamelin Pool Telegraph Station museum. Small white bubbles of oxygen generated by the stromatolite can be seen rising from its upper surface.

184. SILT JETTIES

Of special interest in the Gippsland Lakes is the growth of a birdsfoot delta at the mouth of the Mitchell River where it empties into Lake King south of Bairnsdale. This is the same type of delta as the one where the Mississippi flows into the Gulf of Mexico. Birdsfoot deltas are extremely rare. I know of no other good example in Australia. Most deltas are of the Nile Delta type; triangular in shape with islands filling the gaps between the many distributaries. Birdsfoots only develop where rivers enter shallow lakes or seas where currents are weak or non-existent.

The Mitchell River birdsfoot has only one 'toe' and a short spur. This makes it really easy to explore, particularly as an 8km rough gravel road runs the full length of its southern bank. (If heading south from Bairnsdale towards Paynesville, turn east on the road towards Eagle Point.) Known locally as the Silt Jetties, they are actually levee banks. When a river regularly floods and covers the surrounding land it builds a system of levee banks adjacent and parallel to itself. A fast-flowing flooding river carries large volumes of sand and silt, but where it overflows into already flooded land, or in this case a lake, the speed of flow at the edge of the river slows appreciably which reduces the stream's ability to carry its load of sand and silt. If it can't carry the load it just drops most of it. And where does it drop it? Right where it slows; adjacent to the main stream.

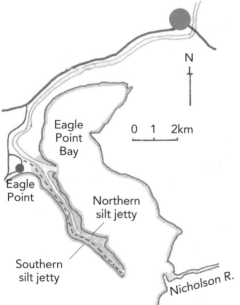

The pair of Mitchell River levees now stretch more than halfway across Lake King. A branching spur is now growing along an opening at the Eagle Point Bay end of the northern levee. The levees were once treed, cleared, and later farmed before being abandoned to anglers. Large rocks have been placed along most of their banks to protect the Silt Jetties from further erosion.

To see real silt drive to the very end of the southern levee, kick the grey/brown crust and it will expose the mottled black silt below.

Central road on the south-eastern Silt Jetty with Lake King on the left and the Mitchell River to the right.

The Mitchell River between its Silt Jetties.

185. SIMPSON DESERT

Row upon row of long, north-south oriented (longitudinal) sand dunes greet four-wheel-drivers as they attempt to cross the Simpson Desert of central Australia. It is thought that the raw materials for these dunes came from the lunettes (ice-age crescent-shaped dunes) that formed around the salt lakes at the northern end of the Flinders Ranges. The main lakes – Torrens, Eyre, Gregory, Blanche and Frome – plus the hundreds of smaller ones developed dunes in the same manner as the Great China Wall that formed at Lake Mungo (**#122**) in New South Wales.

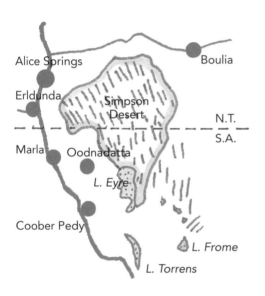

In the lower evaporation times of the ice ages, these lakes filled with water and became permanent. Sandy beaches developed around their shores. The sand was blown into crescent-shaped dunes (hence the name lunette) at the downwind end of each lake.

The lunettes formed mainly on the northern and eastern sides of the southern lakes, the northern side of the central lakes and the north to north-western side of the northern ones. The dominant wind direction at the time of their formation was from the south-west, south and

Simpson Desert after rainstorm.   Photo: Ian Boxall.

south-east respectively. The lunettes provided huge reservoirs of clay, silt and sand. Winds carried much of the lunette raw material in a general northward direction providing the base for the longitudinal dunes.

Like the lunettes, these longitudinal dunes have solid immobile bases covered by layers of sand and clay. In places the crests of these dunes have been breached, exposing unconsolidated sand which is then open to transportation by the wind. This sand, however, does not leave the individual dunes. Eddy currents within these parallel dunes efficiently sweep the sand back into its original dune. The dust has blown away but the sand is fine and soft. The line between the dune base and the swale can be quite sharp.

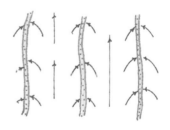

186. STANDLEY CHASM

Standley Chasm has near-vertical parallel sides that lead geologists to conclude that its formation is due to the erosion of a volcanic dyke.

It is thought that dolerite (**#12**) was forced along a joint line in the quartzite at the time the MacDonnell Ranges were forming. The injection filled the joint and forced its sides 4–5m apart. The dolerite then slowly cooled and solidified.

Dolerite is a volcanic rock with a chemical composition the same as basalt. The difference between the two is that basalt flows to and onto the surface where it cools and solidifies. On the other hand, dolerite cools and solidifies below the surface. Due to its slower rate of cooling, dolerite has slightly larger crystals than basalt. Dolerite, like basalt, erodes much faster than quartzite. At around noon, to the satisfaction of visitors, the sun shines almost directly in line with the chasm.

Supporting the conclusion that the chasm marks the prior position of an eroded dyke is the presence of other such dykes in the vicinity of Standley Chasm. An eroding one can be viewed near the road into the chasm. It is located about 100m to the west of the road and starts 6.4km from Namatjira Drive and ends 2.5km from the Standley Chasm Coffee Booth. The dyke is approximately 300m long, 3–4m high and 10–20m wide. Watch out for snakes!

The MacDonnell Ranges are very narrow; less than 10km wide in most places. All of the West MacDonnells are drained by the ancient and only occasionally flowing Finke River (**#72**) and its tributaries.

187. STIRLING RANGES

The Stirling Ranges, only 30km north of the Porongurups (**#171**), has
a shared, but different geological history to its granitic neighbour.
The rocks in the Stirling Ranges began life as sedimentaries and date
back to the time of the Porongurup granite injection. The rocks
were heated and squeezed (metamorphosed) by the granite injection so that the
dominant sandstone became quartzite and the shales became slate. Both quartzite
and slate are far more resistant to erosion than their parents.

More than a billion years later, between 90 million and 50 million years ago,
Australia and Antarctica separated. During the separation Australia pivoted slightly
for a short period, putting extreme compressive pressure on Western Australia's
south-west corner. The Porongurups were squeezed against the older and stronger

Yilgarn craton (**#7**). The Stirling area had nowhere to go other than up. And up it did, forming the Stirling Ranges.

You don't have to climb any of the peaks to take a closer look at the metamorphosed rocks as ample amounts are exposed in road cuttings (above left) leading to Bluff Knoll Lookout (above right).

188. SWANSEA PETRIFIED FOREST

There are very few locations in Australia where you can view
petrified wood in situ. One is at Reid's Mistake near Swansea.
And Reid's 'mistake' had nothing to do with petrified wood. In 1800 Captain
William Reid accidently found himself to be the first European to view what is
now Lake Macquarie. He captained a vessel chartered from Sydney to travel to
Newcastle to bring back a load of coal. Reid mistakenly turned his boat into the
Swansea Channel thinking that he was sailing into the mouth of the Hunter River
at Newcastle. Embarrassing! Left his GPS at home? Even more embarrassing was
that Lake Macquarie was named Reid's Mistake until the lake's name was officially
changed to honour Governor Macquarie in 1826. Reid's name lives on as a small
park on the southern bank of Swansea Channel.

Back to the real story... Petrified wood contains no wood at all. All of the wood
has vanished and been replaced by other minerals; in most cases silica plus some
impurities. The petrified wood at Reid's Mistake and other nearby locations formed
from ancient trees that were blown down by a volcanic explosion that occurred
about 25km to the east, around 250 million years ago. Sea level was lower then.
Following the blast, volcanic dust and ash settled covering the once standing forest.
The trees found themselves in a dark, wet and oxygen-deficient environment. The
volcanic fall-out solidified into a pervious rock called tuff. Water seeping through
the tuff dissolved silica, iron and other impurities from within itself. The dissolved
minerals found their way into the wood's pores and precipitated to fill them. Over
a very long period of time the wood itself was dissolved (not rotted) and filled
with the same cocktail of minerals. Not all of the forest trees were fossilised. Some
became coal by an entirely different process. Coal is a hydrocarbon. There is no
carbon in petrified wood. The process has much in common with the formation
of opal (**#47**). Each fossil site is a shallow depression with what looks like the
rotted base of an electricity pole at its bottom.

Reid's Mistake is reached from the car park at the end of Lambton Parade,
Swansea. Make your way at low tide to the adjacent wave-cut platform at the foot
of Swansea Heads. Exposed tree stumps and some fossilised leaf moulds can be
observed. Other exposures can also be found adjacent to Aldon Crescent, Blackalls
Bay, and at Ghosties Beach, Catherine Hill Bay. Please don't damage or souvenir
the petrified wood.

Opposite below: Rock platform at Swansea Heads.

189. SYDNEY HARBOUR

When viewing Sydney from any vantage point, the bridge and
buildings dominate to such an extent that it is easy to overlook
the fact that you are looking at the lower portion of a valley; the valley of the
Parramatta River. It's hard to imagine that 200 years ago this was a scene of
rolling hills, market gardens and patches of virgin forest. Since that time Sydney's
attractions have been enhanced by the addition of tall buildings, massive bridges
and bright lights; but the real beauty lies in its harbour.

The harbour shares its geological history with that of the Blue Mountains to
the west where the dominant rock is Hawkesbury Sandstone.

When the sandstone was raised above sea level by crustal uplift it cracked,
forming a pattern of joints that run roughly east-west and north-south. The
early Parramatta River followed one of the major east-west joints while its main
tributaries joined from either the north or the south following the other line of
joints. Obvious in today's harbour all the peninsulas, including Milsons Point,
McMahons Point and Darling Point, are aligned north-south. Over the last
2 million years at least four ice-age stages have seen sea level rise and fall each time
by as much as 130m.

During the cold periods the Parramatta River and its tributaries cut valleys deep
into the sandstone and ran along what is now the bottom of Sydney Harbour to
reach the Pacific Ocean 15km or so east of Sydney Heads. The harbour would
have resembled the valleys of the Blue Mountains with towering cliffs at North
Head and South Head marking the edges to the valley. Each time the climate
warmed sea level rose, drowning the lower valley and giving us a Sydney Harbour.
Early Aborigines saw this full cycle at least once.

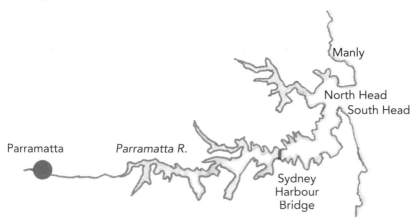

190. TASMAN PENINSULA

The Tasman Peninsula is an inappropriately beautiful setting for some of Australia's most brutal history. It is here that the infamous Port Arthur convict settlement was located, joined to the main island by an easily guarded narrow thread of land surrounded by cliffs and shark-infested

waters. The peninsula contains probably the highest density of superb natural sites to be seen anywhere in the country. These include: the Devils Kitchen, Tasmans Arch (below right), Patersons Arch (below left), the Blowhole, Cape Pillar (opposite above) and the sea stacks at Cape Hauy (bottom).

This concentration of gems is due to the fortuitous juxtaposition of Tasmania's dolerite (**#12**) and its underlying siltstone/ sandstone at sea level where both are attacked by pounding waves. With the dolerite it's not that the waves undercut the cliffs,

but rather that the waves rip out whole chunks of columns near water level so that the now unsupported section above just slides into the sea.

With sandstone and its finer-grained relative, siltstone, it's different. The waves attack paired sets of vertical joint lines. At Patersons Arch, note how the sides of pieces that have fallen away are all close to vertical and you can follow these joints from the sea to the cliff tops.

At Tasmans Arch, processes were similar, but a set of joints on the landward side of the arch were sufficiently weak that a large cavern that had eroded behind the arch was unable to support its roof.

191. TERRIGAL SKILLION

It looks like a cuesta, but it's not. It's just an ordinary hill that's had one end smashed away by ocean waves. A cuesta has a similar look – a hill with one steep slope and one gentle slope as above, but with a cuesta (**#151**) the gentle slope mirrors the slope of the underlying rock. Terrigal's Skillion is built on rock layers that are close to horizontal, hence it does not qualify for any exotic geomorphic title. During the ice ages the Skillion was an ordinary hill with slopes running down from its highest point. When most of the world's ice melted, sea levels rose to cover the mouth of the Hawkesbury River and much of the east coast. What was once a hill became a peninsula jutting out into the Pacific Ocean. Storm waves have eroded away the front half of the peninsula. The rock is not Hawkesbury Sandstone either; it's the rock that lies below Hawkesbury Sandstone. Furthermore, it's not all sandstone.

In the photo (left) you can see three or four thicker bands of pale brown sandstone, but between them are other layers of a greyer colour. Even the sandstone is not just one massive stratum. There's a lot of shale in there, plus some siltstones and mudstones.

These rock strata, the Terrigal Formation, were deposited in very shallow water conditions, possibly river alluvial plains, deltas or even swamps. On the exposed cliff face the lowest layer is shale sitting on top of the more resistant sandstone that now forms the platform that surrounds the cliff. The shale offers much less resistance to the pounding waves and hence undercuts the more resistant sandstone.

The presence of shale in the mix of strata explains why the gentle back slope of the Skillion is so smooth. Soils developed from shale are slippery and prone to sliding downhill covering the bumps and steps that normally occur with changes in rock type.

192. TESSELLATED PAVEMENT

Tasmania's Tessellated Pavement lies only a few kilometres north
of Eaglehawk Neck. It's interesting. It appears as if planned by
a landscape architect and laid by professional bricklayers. It was.
Nature is a great architect and builder. Just look at the quality.

There's more to this site than just the handicraft; it tells a story of erosion. Notice
in the photo (right) that the paving stones closest to the water are rounded on their
tops while the ones closest to land are flatter, even able to hold water. This is rare.

It is called 'loaf and tray' tessellated pavement. The loaf
and tray analogy is quite apt. The geometric pattern was
caused by cracking (jointing). The lines on the surface are
more than lines; they extend down through each stratum
of rock until they reach the next stratum. The loaves (below
centre) are formed by sand and gravel being washed by
breaking waves up and down the lines of cracks. The lines
are abraded more than the blocks by the sand and gravel
because the lines are lines of weakness. Once the grooves
are cut, they become natural channels guiding more and
more of the water, sand and gravel to take this path. It's
not that the loaves rise; it's more that their edges fall.

The trays (below left) are different. They're further
back from the waves. The effect of surging water, gravel and sand is lessened.
The dominant erosional force here is salt. At low tide these rocks are dry, but the
porous sandstone absorbs seawater when covered at high tide. As the water drains
and evaporates, dry salt will show as white lines surrounding rock pools on the
platform. Further drying will lead to salt within the rock precipitating and forming
salt crystals that prise sand grains away from the surface that will be washed away
with the next high tide. The platform edges are mainly dry and made impervious
by the accumulation of iron oxide so that weathering by salt crystallisation is
reduced. Tessellation is relatively common in horizontally bedded sandstone
wave-cut platforms. The example of trays (below right) is at the northern end of
Austinmer Beach, New South Wales.

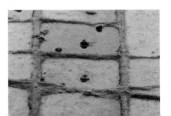

193. THE DRIP

Water dripping from overhanging sandstone is not an unusual or
complex geological phenomenon. In this case however, its setting,
at the end of a 1.2km easy walk from the car park, is spectacular. The Drip is well
signposted from the highway between Mudgee and Merriwa in New South Wales.

The sandstone/conglomerate feature is at the far north-western corner of
the Sydney Basin. Some strata are separated from other strata above by strata
containing impervious clay. Water seeping through the gently dipping sandstone
eventually reach the clay, flow along the top of that stratum to weep out as drips
from the overhanging cliff. A line of moss and/or grass often grows along the
weep line. Even under the severest drought conditions, The Drip continues to drip.

Even without The Drip as prime attraction, the track makes for a great walk.
It runs along the edge of the upper Goulburn River between the river and its

confining cliffs. The path is
reasonably flat and passes via a
footbridge over a small tributary.
Along the way there are fine
examples of conglomerate,
cavernous weathering (**#178**),
cross bedding (**#98**) and even an
archway.

You may be intrigued by
rows of holes in some strata.
The holes have the appearance
of cavernous weathering, but
these cavities have been picked
out by swallows making nests.
Apparently it is easier for the
birds to pick out the holes
than to carry mud and build
conventional nests.

194. THE NUT (CIRCULAR HEAD)

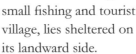

Circular Head, or as it is more commonly known, The Nut, is a promontory that juts out into the western Bass Strait. Stanley, a

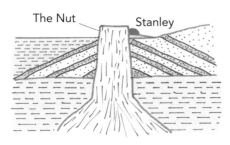

small fishing and tourist village, lies sheltered on its landward side.

Originally The Nut wasn't a promontory; it was a conventional-looking composite volcano many times higher and much broader than it is today. Its sides were composed of alternating lava flows covered by ash and cinder. It was sufficiently large for its apron to extend to higher land in the south and further into Bass Strait to the north. Eruptions ceased around 12.5 million years ago.

Weathering and erosion by wind and rain, assisted by attacks from waves at times of high sea level, has seen the removal of all the ash and lava flows above the current water level. The plug that formed in the volcano's neck is mainly intact. The presence of 140m plunging cliffs in the north, east and west show that the plug has not been immune to attacks by the sea.

The Nut's summit is easily reached by zigzag track or a commercially operated cable car. The top is surprisingly flat, particularly the northern two thirds. It covers 35ha. The centre of the original plug is towards the eastern end of The Nut. A brisk walk around the well-made track takes about 30 minutes. The flatness is thought to be the result of the last eruption being of lava that did not explode over the edge, but settled in the volcano's pipe as a lava lake.

195. THE ROCK

The Rock may be the colloquial name for Uluru in central
Australia, but in New South Wales it's the gazetted name of a
town and its background hill. The Rock is located just south of the city of Wagga
Wagga on the Olympic Highway. There are many other hills in this area, but they
are different; most are granite. You don't get to have a close look at the granite as
road engineers have avoided the granite's steep slopes by following a path along
the gentler slopes and plains that lie between each outcrop. The plains, the granite
and The Rock each belong to different geological episodes. The plain is recent,
formed over the last 40 million to 50 million years; the granites intruded the
Lachlan Folds (**#116**) around 440 million to 420 million years ago; and the Rock's
sedimentaries (sandstones, shales and conglomerates) were laid down on the floor
of a freshwater lake that covered this part of the Lachlan Folds about 400 million
years ago. The original surface has eroded away and is long gone.

A mix of folding and faulting has given The Rock its spectacular shape. The
southern (left) end of the sedimentary is an anticline (upfold) that contrasts with
the near-horizontal main body of the landform. A fault line is present at the break

in slope (right). A shatter zone exists along the fault. A shatter zone is a region where rocks close to a fault line have been broken by the rock movement associated with the earth movement. A gully (above the green tree in the foreground of the bottom image) has formed in this shatter zone.

Steps of alternating cliffs and gentler treed slopes, obvious in all photographs, are the result of alternating strata of resistant sandstone with strata containing some shale.

For a closer view of The Rock, turn into the town from the main highway and follow along the main street that becomes Lockhart Road, then left into the nature reserve. A track leads from the car park up to a viewing platform near the top.

196. THE WALL

The Wall is an inflated basalt ridge 40km long, 20m high and averaging only 70m wide. It sits on top of a near-level lava plain. The top of The Wall is flattish and the sides slope at around 20°(about the same as the slopes of roofs on most houses).

Undara's 'Wall' is the second-longest inflated lava flow in the world. The largest, the Great Basalt Wall (**#74**), is part of a 120km-long lava flow from the Toomba Volcano west of Charters Towers.

Inflation in geologic terms refers to the upward expansion of a contained lava flow. 'The Wall' was initially a long lava flow hemmed between the banks of the Einasleigh River. Overall slope was less than 1°, but the volume of lava was quite huge. The relatively slow-moving lava snout caused lava behind to back up. The top of the flow and its sides cooled relatively quickly forming a thin but solid crust. The crust cracked as it was forced upwards. Leaks appeared, but as they were on the surface, they too quickly solidified. Whole plates moved with the flow. The flow

developed to become an above-ground full lava tube. It only stopped growing when the lava flow ceased.

'The Wall' can be viewed by travelling along O'Briens Creek – Gemfield Road, north-west of the Mount Surprise Township. The road crosses low points in The Wall, 11km from town and again at 33km. Here much better views can be had and the photograph (below) was taken.

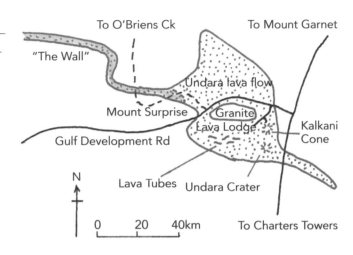

197. THIRLMERE LAKES

Thirlmere Lakes near Picton, New South Wales, are said to be 15 million years old, but they're timeless. Nothing much is happening here.

These lakes formed when the Thirlmere Monocline, an extension of the Lapstone Monocline, became active. Prior to the Thirlmere Monocline, Gum Tree Creek rose at least 20km to the north of the present lakes. The present-day Cedar Creek was the main northern extension of the ancient Gum Tree Creek. Stonequarry and Racecourse Creeks were major tributaries of the Gum Tree.

The Thirlmere Monocline changed all this. The monocline was active along two dimensions; the land to the east of the fold gradually fell, while at the same time the whole area, including the monocline, dipped down towards the north. As these movements were occurring, flow in the northern end of Gum Tree Creek gradually slowed, then ceased. During this period sediment of around 50m in depth was deposited along approximately 10km of the creek bed.

Continued movements along the monocline saw Cedar Creek reverse its direction and, along with other eastern tributaries, flow towards the Nepean River. Two low divides, one just north of Lake Gandangarra and the other just west of Lake Nerrigorang, now leave the lakes in a very small enclosed basin. The lakes are known to have overflowed into the truncated Gum Tree Creek only twice since European settlement, in 1874 and 1974. Water levels can fluctuate between dry and 5m deep. These photographs were taken in 2016 when water levels were low.

Recent research drilling reveals a high congruency between the sediment accumulated at Thirlmere Lakes and those at Lake George (**#120**). The lakes are only 150km apart and have similar climates.

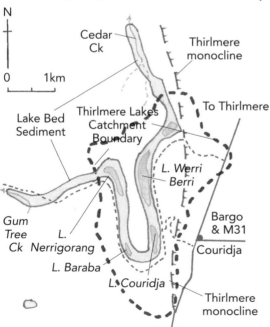

Opposite above: Lake Couridja.
Opposite below: Lake-bed sediment.

198. TOWER HILL

There's no tower and it's not much of a hill. What's more it's in the middle of a lake, but Tower Hill, 14km west of Warrnambool, is a great place to look at volcanic scenery without having to climb mountains or head overseas. You can drive around both its outside and its inside, but better still, there are many paths for you to explore on foot. Tower Hill is a maar (**#16, 150 and 177**), a crater formed

by an explosion of steam caused by rising lava coming in contact with subsurface water. The super-heated water turns to steam blasting the overburden away.

The Tower Hill volcano erupted somewhere around 35,000 years ago and may have formed in less than a year. The crater is near circular and has a diameter of approximately 3km, making it one of the largest maars in the world. The crater floor is 40–50m below the pre-existing ground level. The depth and volume of water in the lake depends upon water supply. In periods of prolonged drought, the lake is reduced to a small area in the south-west. Initially the crater was probably relatively small and only became larger as more water poured from the limestone and onto the magma. As the water supply dwindled,

basaltic lava forced its way up through the accumulated rubble of the crater funnel. The resultant lava fountains built three ash and scoria cones, the highest being Tower Hill.

Eruptions smashed the limestone into mainly dust and sand-sized fragments (above left) that were blasted into the air, only to fall back into and around the crater. The resulting inward-facing steep-sided circular ridge is termed a tuff ring.

Tower Hill was built by a number of eruptions after the initial burst. Its tuff ring was constructed in multiple layers that are exposed

Lava fountain, Yasur, Vanuatu.

in road cuttings and on some of the inward-facing steeper slopes. The most easily viewed are in the disused quarries at the entrance and exit to the Tower Hill Reserve. Much of the ash and dust is off-white to dark grey in colour. Lodged within the ash are blocks of limestone blown out of the previous surface rock by the initial explosion. Holes in the rock are from erosion of the ultra-soft material and are used by birds as condominium nesting sites.

199. TUNNEL CREEK

Tunnel Creek, a tributary of the Lennard River, passes through a
narrow Napier Range ridge in a tunnel. During the dry season the
tunnel can be walked through with the aid of a torch. Tunnels and
caves cut by slightly acidic water are common in limestone (#1).
A walking track down to the tunnel's entrance weaves through fallen slabs and
boulders of limestone that dwarf visitors. Some of the
fallen rocks washed smooth by floods have a mottled
pink colouration (left). This colouring is as old as the
rocks. An ancient form of algae that was trapped during
the formation of the coral reef is responsible for these
patches of colour.

Tunnel Creek ran across the top of the Napier Range
when land surfaces were 50–100m higher in the past. It
was only with the lowering of the surface that the tunnel
began to form. Water commenced seeping along cracks

From the inside looking out.

From the outside, looking in.

within the range. As the land surface fell towards its present level, the creek's waters increasingly passed along these seepage lines eventually coalescing and forming into a tunnel. The abandoned valley of the creek's original course can be seen above its present subterranean course.

Tunnel Creek's entrance is invitingly sandy and reassuringly well used.

Bring a good torch; it's a 1.5km return trip. Also, wear sneakers as you have to scramble over rocks that have fallen from the roof and wade through permanent pools of cold water.

332

200. TWELVE APOSTLES

There's a fair amount of licence in the naming of these stacks as the Twelve Apostles. Most people see eight, but others see nine. The ninth is simply a stump of a stack. The large stack (opposite) has been undercut and will eventually fall (possibly in your lifetime) and erode away. But don't worry – all the nearby headlands are the Apostles of the future.

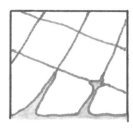 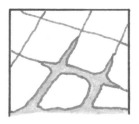

The Twelve Apostles' section of coast consists almost entirely of very young limestone. Around 20 million years ago a shallow sea that teemed with calcium-rich algae, shellfish and bryozoans covered this area of southern Victoria. Bryozoans, small 1–2mm-sized aquatic animals, like corals, lived in communities. When bryozoans died they disintegrated into fine grains of calcium. These calcium-rich layers compacted under their own weight and cemented together to form limestone.

About 5 million years ago the land rose and the seabed became dry land. During the uplift the limestone was cracked with major joint lines running from south-west to north-east. This influenced the shape of many of the headlands and islands in the area.

201. TYTO WETLANDS

Tyto is the scientific name of a native bird, the Eastern Grass Owl, that inhabits, in limited numbers, this restored wetland on the Herbert River Delta just a few hundred meters from Ingham's main street. The Herbert Delta is of the common triangular shape, with its apex inland, north-west of the town. Its other defining points are the mainland adjacent to the southern end of Hinchinbrook Island in the north-east and Halifax Bay National Park in the south-east. To study this delta there is an advantage in exploring the restoration at the Tyto Wetlands over the more pristine Halifax Bay NP; Tyto is accessible.

Deltas are floodplains formed at the mouths of rivers that empty into stillish waters. The Herbert drains part of Australia's highest rainfall area. It falls dramatically from the nearby mountains onto the coastal plain where deposition becomes the prime feature of the landscape. River channels are regularly blocked by silt. New channels are easily cut through the soft deposits, but have an uncertain future. The main stream becomes braided and its flow reduced as distributaries (**#134**) leave the stream to make independent paths to the sea.

Tyto wetlands were initially covered by forest, cleared, artificially drained then planted with sugarcane. Restoration has seen the farming cease, artificial drainage blocked or removed and some replanting of the natural vegetation. The wetland is now criss-crossed by well-made paths, bridges over former distributaries and raised boardwalks. Deep waterholes, once oxbow lakes (billabongs), are now teeming with waterbirds.

202. UCONTITCHIE HILL

There are a number of 'Rocks' and 'Hills' in the northern Eyre Peninsula. Among them are Minnipa Hill, Pildappa Rock and Ucontitchie Hill (bottom). They provide the best examples of granite shapes and forms that the author has ever seen, anywhere.

Such low hills are called inselbergs from the German *Insel*, meaning island, and *berg*, meaning mountain. Ucontitchie Hill is great – it's reasonably easy to climb if you start from the southern edge near the water pipe, and it is not all that hard to pronounce either. Try it slowly: 'you-con-teach-e'. Ucontitchie Hill is about 30km south-west of Wudinna along a good gravel road. It stands out on the sand plain like the hull of an upturned boat in an ocean of wheat stubble. The hill is on private land, but has a dedicated parking lot, information signs, tracks and an honesty box to hold 'gold' coin donations to defray expenses.

The main bulk of Ucontitchie has good examples of sheet structure (**#55** and opposite centre) where large slabs of the surface are separating from the

underlying main body of granite. Another great example of this feature can also be seen at the left end of the hill shown in the photo at the bottom of the page. The hill also has magnificent examples of flared slopes (**#210** and *opposite centre*).

The crest of Ucontitchie looks likes nature's attempt at Stonehenge. It's a little flatter up there, some soil has not washed away, and hardy shrubs grow. The tors and pillars are remnants of a former sheet that is eroding, weathering and decomposing towards oblivion. Over the next millions of years, the nearly-solid top layer will repeat the same processes.

203. ULLADULLA PLATFORM

Ulladulla is a popular holiday town on the south coast of New South Wales. It boasts three attractions of special interest: fossil museum, geological time walk and escorted fossil walk. The museum is small, but great; the time walk is self-guiding through Brodie Park, viewing rocks of the area laid out in chronological order; but it's Ulladulla's fossil walk that I'll concentrate on.

You can do this walk by yourself at no cost and at any time when the tide permits, but it's best to go with a guide. Check on the internet for dates, times and booking procedures (small fee applies). The guide will lead you to the fossils, most of which are small. Once your eyes become accustomed to fossil spotting, you will have little difficulty in identifying many more. The fossil on the left is of a bivalve mollusc *Pecten* shell. This genus includes pippis and scallops. It is also used as a logo by a well-known petroleum company. The fossils below are of sea fans, members of the bryozoan family that resemble soft corals, while the one opposite above is of a spirifer, a hard-shelled brachiopod.

The siltstone rock in which the fossils are housed was deposited as fine sediment around 270 million years ago in the middle of the Permian period of geological time. Hence these fossils are often referred to as 'Permian Fossils'. Over a period of just 4 million years, around 180m of deposition took place here.

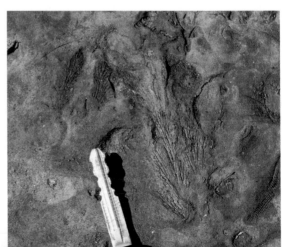

But not all things of interest in these rocks are fossils. You should look for dropstones (**#209**) and Glendonites (*below*). Glendonites are clusters of the crystal Ilkaite ($CaCO_36H_2O$). These crystals only grow in water where temperatures are less than 5°C. Only a few of these crystal clusters can be found on the fossil walk.

204. ULURU AND MOUNT CONNER

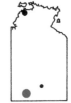

Uluru, 'The Rock', an Australian icon, is not a conventional rock with a top, bottom and sides. You can't dig under it or with some giant machine, lift it up and lay it on the surface. It is not a rock in that sense at all; it's a remnant of an ancient mountain upfold. Uluru stands nearly 350m above the surrounding plain. The perimeter of the 'rock' at ground level is 9.4km, its length 3.6km and width 1.9km.

Mount Conner, 100km east of Uluru, is an unlikely looking sibling to the star Central Australian attraction. Both are sculptured from sandstone and are of similar size, altitude, height above surrounding land and area. Mount Conner is approximately 3km long and 2.5km wide. But that's where all similarity ends.

Mount Conner is a flat-topped mesa surrounded by 100m cliffs and a smothering skirt of talus. Uluru is a great big blob of rock that glows red in the setting sun.

Both had their beginnings as sand washed into a sea from nearby ancient mountains that existed in this area 500 million to 600 million years ago. The sand and gravel comprised mainly quartz crystals and granite pebbles together with small amounts of clay and iron. These ingredients were slowly compressed to form sandstone and/or conglomerate. Between 340 million and 310 million years ago these sedimentary strata were uplifted at the same time as compression from the north and south forced the land to rise. Under increasing pressure, some areas started to fold and fracture along lines of weakness. One of the numerous lines of weakness was in the Uluru – Kata Tjuta area and another in the McDonnell Ranges.

The rock strata, that later became Uluru, lay on the north side of the sharp east-west Uluru-Kata Tjua anticline (upfold) that developed. These strata were inclined to near vertical (right). Stronger strata nearby such as in the vicinity of Mount Conner remained untouched and close to horizontal. Rocks at the top of the anticline were shattered and have eroded away. Those at the bottom are covered by the eroded sand and gravel from the anticline. Uluru strata, although tilted, remained mainly unbroken and now stand out as a remnant floating in a sea of sand that it helped create (below).

205. UNDARA LAVA TUBES

The lava tubes at Undara are considered to be the finest and
longest examples of lava tubes in the world. A lava tube is a
self-made natural tunnel through which lava flows. These tubes
generally develop in lava flowing down a boiled out stream
bed. If the lava is not turbulent, the crust may solidify from contact with the air
while the lava below continues to flow. Once commenced, the tubes continue

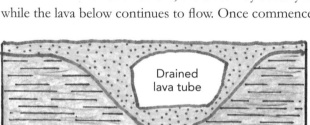

Drained
lava tube

to grow in length as
the solidified roof
insulates the flowing
lava beneath from the
cooling effect of the
air above. The drop in
temperature of lava
flowing within a tube
can be as little as 1°C for every kilometre travelled. When the eruption ceases the
tube will continue to drain until the flow's snout solidifies. The thickness of lava
tubes' roofs varies, but can be as little as 1–2m (opposite, below).

The unspectacular Undara Volcano had a one-off eruption about 190,000
years ago. This eruption spewed 23 cubic kilometres of basaltic lava onto the
surrounding land. That's nearly 50 Sydney Harbours if you are familiar with Sydney
Harbour. The eruption initially produced a lava plain to the north of the eruption
centre (**#196**), but on reaching the headwaters of the Einasleigh River in the west
and the Lind River in the east all additional lava was channelled down the valleys
of the two streams. The Einasleigh Flow was 160km long and the Lynd 100km.

The length and efficiency of the flow was assisted by a number of factors.
The land was almost flat from earlier older lava flows from nearby volcanoes;

the lava was very hot,
probably 1,200°C to 1,300°C
and extremely liquid; the
two rivers provided pre-
existing channels for the
lava to flow in, and the flow
was continuous and of large
volume. Land above the
tubes is quite flat (left).

206. WESTERN AUSTRALIA'S INTER-CRATON SMALL FOSSILS

Western Australia is a huge state, but much of it is fossil free. Many of its large regions are covered by ancient rocks that predate life on Earth while others are covered by sand. However, one area worth exploring is the narrow stretch that separates the Yilgarn and Pilbara Cratons (**#7**). The basement rock here is also very old, but it has been raised and lowered several times and is now covered by a variety of younger sedimentary deposits. It is in these younger rocks that some fossils are located.

One important fossil site is located in the Kalbarri National Park. The fossil (opposite above) is not of an animal, rather it's the tracks made by an animal around 400 million years ago. This amphibious animal, a eurypterid, was somewhat like a lobster-sized scorpion. It moved from waterhole to waterhole. Its tracks were covered by silt during a flooding event. Erosion has removed the siltstone and exposed the tracks in the more resistant sandstone. The tracks are located just 20m from the Z Bend Viewing Platform and are clearly signposted.

Another fossil site worth viewing in the inter-craton zone lies beside the Cobra–Mount Augusta road north-east of Kalbarri. The fossils fragments (opposite below) here are from brachiopods, bryozoans, crinoids and nautiloids. The fossils are around 100 million years younger than those at Kalbarri and formed while the area was submerged beneath the ocean. The now uplifted limestone rock is

referred to as the Callytharra Formation. This stratum is approximately 200m thick with fossils spread throughout.

The site has an information board and the road is useable in dry weather.

207. WABMA KADARBU MOUND SPRINGS

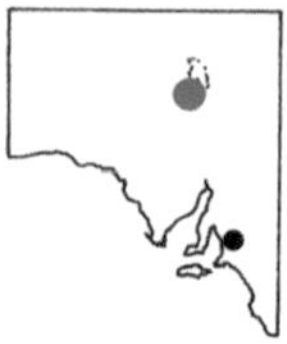

Looking like small volcanic cones, the Wabma Kadarbu Mound Springs are located along a gravel road that runs south from the Oodnadatta Track, 6km east of Cameron Springs. Unfortunately, most traffic on the Oodnadatta Track bypasses the mound springs to head to the Cameron Springs

which are not springs at all. The so called Cameron Springs is a bore that was sunk in 1886 during the construction of the original Ghan Rail line. The springs at Wabma Kadarbu are both real and fascinating.

Wabma Kadarbu Mound Springs are a natural outlet for the Great Artesian Basin (**#88**). This basin, one of the largest groundwater basins in the world, was formed between 250 million and 60 million years ago, a period when down-warping of the area led rivers to flow into the basin from the east and west carrying huge quantities of sand, gravel and finer materials such as silt and clay. As the weight of sediment increased, the geologic basin sank to greater and greater depths. The deepest layers of sediment are now more than 3,000m below the surface. Most of the fresh water enters the aquifers where they outcrop on the western side of the Great Dividing Range. It is estimated that the basin is capable of holding enough water to fill Sydney Harbour 130,000 times over. The water

moves down through the sandstones at a rate of around 3–4m a year. In areas such as Wabma Kadarbu, water flows to the surface along fault or joint lines. Water at Wabma Kadarbu has been dated by scientists at about 2 million years of age.

Natural outlets are surrounded by low mounds formed from very fine sediment carried to the surface in the water. The artesian water also contains small quantities of mineral impurities that make it 'tasty' to humans but still suitable for cattle and sheep. The presence of sodium in the water makes it unsuitable for large-scale irrigation of crops. Clusters of salt crystals (opposite above) are found on the skirts of some springs where seepage takes place through their sides.

208. WALLAMAN FALLS

Wallaman Falls, east of Ingham in northern Queensland, has the longest straight drop (305m) of any waterfall in Australia. The falls are on Stony Creek, a tributary of the east-flowing Herbert River.

Long before the development of the falls, the Herbert River flowed north-west to enter the ocean in the vicinity of what is now the Gulf of Carpentaria. Uplift to the north of Hughenden around 8 million years ago tilted the land surface sufficiently to reverse the flow of the Herbert and make it flow south, then east, to empty into the Coral Sea. Being in Australia's highest rainfall area and having quite an extensive drainage basin, the Herbert River quickly cut a deep gorge back into the freshly uplifted Great Dividing Range. Stony Creek with its much smaller drainage catchment was unable to match the Herbert's down-cutting ability and found itself suspended above it, joining the mainstream via a precursor Wallaman Falls. The falls have gradually moved upstream, cutting a gorge that in parts is over 500m deep. Headward progress of the fall has been slow through the ancient volcanic rhyolite and trachyte rocks over which it flows. The 20m-deep plunge pool at the foot of the falls continually undercuts the cliff behind the falls and should ensure that the falls, even as they continue to migrate upstream, will remain spectacular for quite a few more million years.

The gravel/partly sealed road leading to the falls is suitable for most domestic vehicles, but caravans are not recommended as parts of the road are narrow and used by commercial logging trucks. At the top of the falls there is a campground, a parking area for day-trippers, toilets, water and a 300m-long, wheelchair-friendly path from the car park to a viewing platform from which these photographs were taken. A path from the car park leads to the foot of the falls. It's the same distance coming back as going down, but few who have made the journey believe this. If the sun is shining, you may find a brilliant rainbow formed across the falls.

209. WASP HEAD

The beauty of Wasp Head is that it has a huge variety of nature's specials within 100m of each other, and it is easy to get to. Drive to Murramarang along South Durras Road; follow the road around to the Murramarang Resort, pass between the resort and its parking area, immediately turn left and follow the short gravel road to its end above Wasp Head. From the parking area walk east a couple of hundred metres towards the headland then take any one of the tracks leading south-east down to the beach. Once on the beach, turn left and walk towards the headland. Mark on the beach where you came out of the low forest; it makes it easier to find your way back to the car.

Almost as you step onto the beach you are greeted by a lattice-like formation consisting of ribs made from what looks like rusty iron. This is boxwork, and it is rusty iron. Iron and silica have been delivered to these sites dissolved in

groundwater. Iron rich water seeps down through the rocks and eventually percolates to the surface along joint lines and through other porous lines in the sandstone. As the water evaporates it leaves deposits of iron oxide (rust) and silica. These deposits are much harder and more resistant to erosion than their sandstone host. The sandstone is eroded away by salt wedging (**#192**), and the abrasive action of loose stones and gravel trapped within the framework and moved around by wind and wave action.

By this time you will have already noticed the dropstones; one was at your feet while you were examining the boxwork. Dropstones were left here by melting icebergs nearly 400 million years ago.

The goodies continue. Keep walking towards the headland with your head down. You're looking for something that looks like a rusty iron bar. It may even be covered by water. It's not an iron bar, but it does have a connection with the iron boxwork. The same iron oxide and silica found in the boxwork has in this case entered the pores of a fallen giant tree fern totally replacing the original material and forming the equivalent of fossilised wood (**#188**).

Keep looking down, you can't miss this one; a slash of different rock cutting north-south across the sandstone platform and into the peninsula. It's a volcanic dike. About 30 million years ago, liquid basalt magma was injected with such pressure into a joint line that it split the sandstone and forced the two sections apart. The basalt cooled and solidified. There's an odd thing about basalt. It's harder than sandstone, but where there's moisture around, it disintegrates, weathers and erodes much faster than its 'soft' neighbour. Note in the photo (below) the gap where the basalt has been completely eroded away just where it enters the ocean while the sandstone has resisted the onslaught of the waves.

210. WAVE ROCK

Not seen in many photos of Wave Rock, is the low thin concrete wall that winds its way across the Rock's top. The wall diverts water from running down the rock and directs its flow instead into a small reservoir. This is probably as close as it gets to there being a wave at Wave Rock.

Wave Rock is solid granite. Granite was first injected into south-west WA about 2.7 billion years ago, making it more than half the age of the Earth. This huge body of granite is one of the anchors of the Australian Continent (**#7**). But the granite at Hyden is much younger. Around 500 million years ago, a second, smaller body of molten granite was forced through a break in the older granite to settle, cool and solidify above it, but below layers of existing sedimentary rock.

Over the next 400 million years the overlying sedimentary rock has eroded away, eventually exposing the younger granite. Wave Rock and numerous other granite domes in the

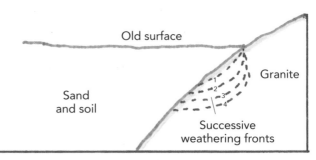

area are the upper surface of the now partly exposed younger granite intrusion. The exposed surface of Hyden Rock has continued to slowly erode while the surface of the surrounding countryside has been spasmodically lowered.

Technically, wave-shaped rocks are flared slopes. Such landforms are common in the south-west of Western Australia and also in the northern Eyre Peninsula of South Australia. An unusual element regarding the creation of such landforms is that they are shaped entirely below the land surface and become exposed only after the local surface has been lowered by erosion.

Water running off the surface of exposed granite flows

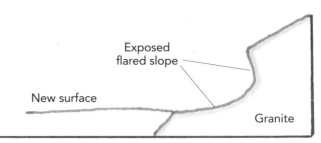

over its edges and seeps into the adjacent sub-surface. It's not the action of the running water that's responsible for the rock's shape, it's the slow weathering of the hidden granite that lies below that surface. Water and oxygen react with the granite's feldspar crystals to form clay. Clay expands when wet and shrinks as it dries. Such movement is sufficient to loosen quartz crystals, the other major component of granite. This process has been described by some as rotting, and may lead to granite surfaces that alternate between wet and dry, disintegrating at a faster rate than surfaces that are continually dry or wet. The diagrams (opposite) illustrate how the alternating wet-dry 'solid' granite eventually disintegrates into sand and clay exposing a fresh weathering front for the water to continue its attack.

Eventually, another wave shape may form that is exposed only if and when there is a lowering of the surrounding land surface. How long does this take? A very long time!

211. WELLINGTON CAVES

Wellington Caves are much the same age as other limestone cave systems in New South Wales. This is to be expected as all their limestones were developed at a time when much of New South Wales lay beneath a shallow warm sea. Wellington's limestone is 386 million to 390 million years old and predates the uplifting of the Great Dividing Range by squillions of years. The caves are neither as magnificent nor as extensive as those at Jenolan, nor are they as artistically lit, but they have some other real advantages as far as visitors are concerned. They contain a brilliant array of fossils, some great history and are so easy to get to. Found in gently rolling hills, close to a major country town and served by sealed main roads that lead right up to the cave steps, these caves are certainly more accessible than their better-known rivals. You are

not overwhelmed by bus-loads of tourists or a bewildering range of tours, times and prices. The phosphate mine section of the cave system is even wheelchair accessible.

There are three cave sections open to guided tours: Cathedral Cave, Gaden Cave and the Phosphate Mine and Fossil Caves. The Cathedral and Gaden Caves have a good range of common limestone speleothems such as stalagmites, stalactites, columns, flutes, curtains and shawls. The Cathedral Cave, as its name suggests, is large and has several special features. The Cathedral's centrepiece, The Altar (opposite), is part of a very, very large stalagmite. It weighs thousands of tonnes and is large enough to claim the title as the largest stalagmite in Australia. Not only is it big, it's spectacular.

One of the caves was mined for phosphate during World War I as Australia's main supplier of this fertilizer – the island of Nauru was at that time owned by the Germans. The current entrance to the mine cave was dug by the miners to facilitate their mining activities, but before that it was open to the outside via a sink hole. The sink hole provided entry for the bats, but was also a trap for animals that stumbled into it. Dead animal bodies were washed further into the caves during flood times. Here they became embedded and fossilised in guano and alluvium.

Once visitors pass through the old mining section they are led to the most interesting part of the cave; the fossil beds. Many of the fossils may be handled.

212. WILPENA POUND

Parts of the Flinders Ranges in South Australia could rightfully be referred to as the upside-down ranges. Not that they have been literally turned upside down, but in some areas the landscape has been reversed. What were once hills are now valleys and beside them are hills that were once ancient valleys. Wilpena Pound is one of the world's finest examples of this phenomenon.

The reversal of hills into valleys is the result of extremely rapid erosion of the anticlines (upfolds) following their shattering during formation. As they were squeezed and pushed up, the top layers stretched to the point where they broke, forming deep V-shaped cracks that extended well into the underlying strata. As the folding took millions of years, the cracks had ample time to partially fill with eroded rock and earth. These cracks and their loosely compacted fill allowed water and air to penetrate so that the tops of the anticlines became easy targets for the forces of erosion. The bottoms of the synclines (downfolds) were subject to different pressures. The folding compressed these layers making them harder and more resistant and closed to penetration by air and water. Erosion at the base of the synclines was extremely slow.

As erosion proceeded, the surface level of the upfolds eventually fell below that of the downfolds. The resistant lower walls of the synclines now stand out as ridges and the bottoms have become perched valleys or pounds. Some estimate up to 6,000m has been eroded from the tops of the anticlines to give us the present-day low mountains. From the east, outside the pound, the edge of Wilpena is an imposing buttress with St Mary Peak (centre) the highest point in the Flinders Ranges.

Wilpena Pound.   Photo: Alan Moore.

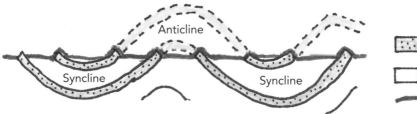

Anticline

Syncline   Syncline

213. WINDJANA GORGE

The entry (opposite, below) is spectacular, the scenery even more
so. It's one of the author's favourites. The gorge is short – only
3.5km long. It contains all the usual Kimberley limestone features of

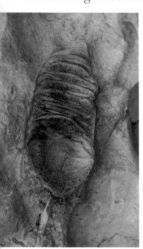

streaked and fluted rocks and orange splashed,
colourful sheer cliffs. Noisy corellas share the trees with
fruit bats and tourist-friendly Freshwater Crocodiles warm
themselves on the sandy beaches.

For those wanting to further enhance their knowledge,
and for something different, there's a wonderful fossilised
nautiloid exposed on the wall of the gorge. The fossil is
approximately 22cm long and is clearly signposted.

The Napier Range Reef (opposite) through which the
Lennard River has cut the gorge is unlike present-day reefs.
This reef was built mainly from algae and other lime-
excreting organisms more so than coral. The reefs consisted
of numerous isolated atolls and extensive barrier chains,
some more than 100km long. During the reef's growing

years, the sea floor gradually fell, but
the reef-building organisms grew
and died at the same rate, building
limestone that reached a depth of an
incredible 2,000m in places. About
100 million years later the sea floor
rose exposing the reefs to the surface.
This was followed by a further period
of subsidence when the reefs fell
below sea level and became covered
by sandstones and mudstones.
About 20 million years ago the area
was again uplifted and subjected to
erosion. All the young sandstones and
mudstones have eroded away along
with the upper layers of the older
rock that had not been colonised by
the lime-excreting organisms.

214. WOMBEYAN CAVES

Wombeyan has something special in its craybacks. There's also one at the Abercrombie Caves, but nowhere as obvious or as well formed as the three at the entrance to Wombeyan's Fig Tree Cave. They're not all that pretty, but if they look like lobster tails they have appeal.

Craybacks are a type of stalagmite that may form at a cave's entrance. The one in the photo (below) is about perfect. It is located in a near-ideal position. The roof, the source of the calcite laden drips, is high; the cave is a tunnel with winds that blow, at different times, either in or out of the entrance; and thirdly, direct sunlight strikes part of the crayback.

Here's how it works. With a roof height in excess of 20m, even a slight breeze can cause a falling drip to veer off vertical by several metres, but only along an axis parallel to the wind direction. Hence the feature is much longer than it is wide.

The sunlit end of a crayback is covered by algae (cyanobacteria) which use sunlight to consume carbon dioxide for photosynthesis.

As the carbon dioxide is consumed, the drip's calcite is precipitated causing the stalagmite to grow upward and also towards the sunlight. The crenulated tail consists of raised ribs that catch the high sun of summer, but shade and slow the growth of older ribs further down the tail.

This cave system has evolved in marble, an uncommon rock in Australia. Marble is much harder than limestone, but like limestone, is dissolvable by weak acids. Wombeyan's limestone was laid down in a shallow sea around 410 million years ago, but was later heated from below by the intrusion of granite, and from above by lava flows from the nearby Yerranderie Volcano. Fig Tree Cave is regarded by many as the best self-guided cave tour in New South Wales.

The water sculptured entry/exit is spectacular (opposite, below). At flood times the creek can become a rushing turbulent torrent more than 5m deep. The main chambers within the cave are huge and the lighting is good.

215. WOOLSHED CREEK FOSSILS

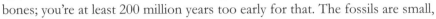

The ACT boasts one the best Silurian (around 400 million years ago) fossil sites in the country. Don't expect to find dinosaur bones; you're at least 200 million years too early for that. The fossils are small,

but once you find one and know what you're looking for; it's not difficult to find quite a few more. The site, where Fairburn Avenue crosses Woolshed Creek near the airport, mainly contains brachiopod, but also some bryozoan, trilobite and coral fossils.

Brachiopods (left) are bivalve shellfish. These fleshy invertebrates lived enclosed between two

hinged shells. When alive, the Brachiopods at Woolshed Creek, belonging to the species *Atrypa duntroonis*, were around 20–25mm in diameter. It is thought that this collection was ripped from their anchors during storm times, smashed and later washed into stiller water and covered by fine silt. Most are not true fossils, but rather moulds of the shells made before their eventual dissolution. This is similar to the formation of fish fossils at Canowindra (**#3**). You may have to look very carefully to find some of the smaller fossils at the site. Some are given away by colour and others by shape.

The rock containing the fossils (below) is a mudstone deposited in a shallow marine environment that existed in the area at that time.

The site is at a busy road and interchange, so it's best to park at the Duntroon Cricket Ground at the end of Hopkins Road and walk the newly constructed path to Woolshed Creek and under the bridge to the site. Here you will find an information board that gives details of the site and its discovery.

216. WINEGLASS BAY

There's more to Freycinet than Wineglass Bay; but it's the jewel that attracts visitors to the peninsula. Once there, they discover much more to see and do. There are many ways to view this gem; fly, arrive by tour boat, or best of all walk through a gap in The Hazards (below) to a viewing point overlooking the tombolo. Yes, that's what Wineglass Bay is; it's a tombolo (**#23**); a deposit of sand joining an island to the mainland.

Freycinet is one of a series of French place names found along the southern coast of Australia from Tasmania to Fremantle. Louis-Claude Freycinet was chief surveyor and cartographer for the French expedition that explored the coast in the ships *Le Geographe* and *Le Naturaliste* in 1802–03. Freycinet discovered that the peninsula which now bears his name was in fact a peninsula and not a string of islands as had been previously thought.

At a width of 1.5km, this tombolo is wider than most. The presence of separate sand-dune systems on each side and the lagoon between them indicates that the tombolo has continued to grow after its initial formation. Prior to the development of the tombolo a broad channel separated the Hazards from the

Wineglass Bay.   Photo: Ian Boxall.

remainder of the peninsula to the south. Waves from the south swept sand along both sides of the peninsula, converged in the middle of the channel and dropped their loads there. The waves were larger on the exposed eastern beach; consequentially the accumulation of sand on that side is greater.

The Hazards.

217. WILSONS PROMONTORY

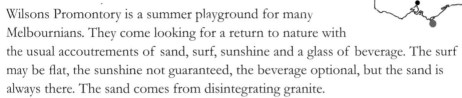

Wilsons Promontory is a summer playground for many
Melbournians. They come looking for a return to nature with
the usual accoutrements of sand, surf, sunshine and a glass of beverage. The surf
may be flat, the sunshine not guaranteed, the beverage optional, but the sand is
always there. The sand comes from disintegrating granite.

The granite welled up beneath the pre-existing rocks of the area around 400
million years ago. It was kilometres below the surface and formed a huge body of
rock termed a batholith that extends from Wilson's Promontory south and into
north-eastern Tasmania. Since that time, uplift and erosion have seen the removal
of the overlying strata, the exposure of the granite and extensive erosion of the
granite itself.

Some geologists believe that The Prom oscillated between being a peninsula
and an island many times during the ice ages. In cold times when sea level fell by
as much as 130m, it was joined to Tasmania by dry land, but became an island
separated from the Australian mainland by shallow water as sea levels rose at the
end. At the end of the ice age sea-levels were slightly above those existing today.
The Prom may well have been an island at that time. The abundance of sand,
favourable ocean currents and the sheltered nature of the coast north of the
Wilsons Promontory Island, however, led to the development of a broad sand spit
rejoining it to the mainland and creating Corner Inlet.

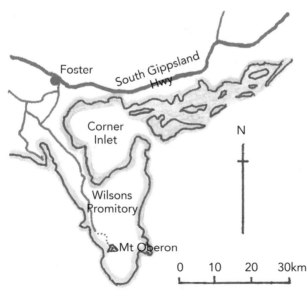

Bare granite is
exposed on the tops and
sides of large domes
such as Mounts Oberon,
Bishop, Wilson, Vereker,
Latrobe and others, and
on coastal headlands.
The photos (opposite)
were taken to the
south-west from Mount
Oberon, the most easily
accessed peak on the
Prom.

218. WOLF CREEK CRATER

Wolf Creek is not the largest of Australia's meteor craters – Lake Acraman in South Australia and Gosse Bluff in the Northern Territory are both bigger – but it's certainly the most spectacular.

About 2 million years ago a small meteor struck the Earth at Wolf Creek, blasting a crater that is now 60m deep and 850m wide. The rim of the crater, pushed up by the impact, rises 35m above the surrounding plain. On an inverted five-point scale, it has the highest classification as a crater, with category 1. Category 1 craters are those that contain fragments of the original meteor. There are only 12 of this category known on Earth and Wolf Creek is the second largest. The crater was at least twice as deep when formed, but has since partially filled with eroded sand and rock from the crater walls and surrounding semi-desert. Most of the excavated rock was pulverised by the impact and thrown into the atmosphere from where it was carried away by blast-generated winds. Some heavier fragments, however, fell around the crater edge helping build the raised ridge that surrounds the huge hole in the ground.

Other easily viewed craters in Australia include Hendbury (**#96**) and Gosse Bluff (**#86**), both in the Northern Territory.

Photos: Chris and Judy Pratt

219. WOLLOMOMBI FALLS

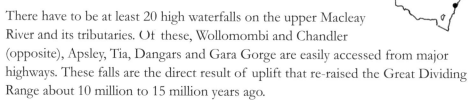

There have to be at least 20 high waterfalls on the upper Macleay River and its tributaries. Of these, Wollomombi and Chandler (opposite), Apsley, Tia, Dangars and Gara Gorge are easily accessed from major highways. These falls are the direct result of uplift that re-raised the Great Dividing Range about 10 million to 15 million years ago.

Prior to uplift, the New England area was an area of gently undulating hills. Its altitude was between 200–300m and its rivers drained to the Pacific Ocean in the east. As the Dividing Range rose the Upper Macleay land surface was lifted by some 500–800m. What had been a gently flowing Macleay River system became, in part, a raging torrent cascading over rapids with waterfalls quickly creating new landscapes.

This change in river behaviour is termed rejuvenation and sparks a fresh cycle of erosion. Erosion is most rapid where streams run fastest, so it was along the new eastern-facing escarpment that the freshly raised Dividing Range was attacked. As waterfalls erode their beds, the falls move upstream. The plunging water erodes a deep pool at the base of the fall by initiating shock waves that cause the submerged rock to gradually disintegrate. Gravel and boulders washed down by the stream accelerate this process. Parts of the cliff fall in and the falls move a little further upstream. Over and over this process is repeated with cliffs falling and rocks disintegrating and wearing away.

This set of Macleay River falls have travelled upstream more than 200km in the past 15 million years. When the migrating falls reach a river junction, they simply split and continue to move up each tributary. The Wollomombi and Chandler falls are of the same age, as are the Tia and Apsley falls. The Wollomombi is a

tributary of the Chandler and the Tia is a tributary of the Apsley River. Both the Chandler and Apsley Rivers are tributaries of the Macleay. All of these falls, plus others, started as a single fall on the Macleay River just upstream from Kempsey. The Wollomombi-Chandler pair of falls are of special interest, not only because they are the highest in the region at 220m, but also because they illustrate perfectly the splitting of a waterfall to become twins, after reaching a point where a river divides. Chandler Falls (left, and top right in image opposite) are more fragmented than their sibling, Wollomombi Falls.

Photo: Shutterstock | THP Creative

220. WORM-TUBE FOSSILS

If you stay in Kalbarri you might like to go looking for fossilised
worm tubes. There are plenty around. I found some just a few
kilometres south of town. Drive to the end of Rainbow Valley Road,
then start walking the track from Rainbow Valley to Mushroom Rock.
After only a couple of hundred metres the track heads down a short, steep, but
easily negotiated incline. Head down for a dozen steps, turn around and look back
and you will see hundreds of fossilised worm tubes.

    If you enjoy fishing you may wish you had access to such large worms today.
The worms that lived in these tubes must have been 1m or more long and up to

5cm thick; about the size of a typical snake. What great bait. The worms lived in the sediment of a shallow sea around 400 million years ago. They dug vertical holes into the sea-floor sediment and used these holes as homes and as protection from predators. When the worms died or abandoned their homes the holes filled with fresh sediment of a different texture to that of the original. Both the original sediment and the abandoned worm tubes were covered by additional sediment that compressed them into a weak sandstone. Remarkably these fossils are not far from their original environment. They have been exposed by storm waves washing up an inclined rocky platform. The tube sediment has proved to be more resistant to erosion than that around it and hence the tubes now stand out as thin vertically aligned cylinders. Broken cylinders can be seen lying on flat ledges (opposite, below).

221. YARRANGOBILLY CAVES

Jersey Cave, one of four caves open to the public at Yarrangobilly, is certainly the most interesting limestone cave the author has ever visited, and also one of the prettiest.

There's abundant limestone dotted around within the Kosciuszko National Park. The Yarrangobilly chunk is fairly large; 14km long and 1.5km wide. The rock is 440 million years old, but the caves are much younger. It was only 40 million years ago that this area was uplifted out of the ocean. Jersey Cave only commenced forming 750,000 years ago.

To gain prominence among speleologist aficionados, caves must have something special to lift their appeal. Jersey Cave has two such features – black flowstones (left) and dogtooth spars (below).

The most compelling explanation I have found for the black/grey colouring of some flowstones and other features is that it comes from ash brought into the caves following bushfires. The same acidic water that carries dissolved limestone also carries the undissolved fine ash and soot. This carbon eventually settles on surfaces only to be covered by the translucent calcite. A well-credentialed source claims that the cave provides the longest continuous history of bushfires at any one site in Australia.

The dogtooth spars are even more fascinating. The 'spar' bit is a generalised term for glass-like crystals. The 'dogtooth' is a simple descriptor; it is pointy and looks somewhat like a dog's tooth. It doesn't sound like a scientific term, but it is.

Dogtooth spars develop in rimstone pools. These isolated pools of water are held in place by calcite walls that have formed where calcium-saturated water spills or seeps over a pool's edge (#124). Under drying conditions, a pool may lose some of its CO_2 directly to the atmosphere causing its calcite load to precipitate as a clear scum. Some of the minute calcite crystals may coalesce, forming a nucleus to which other crystals are attracted and grow. Some of these crystals grow to lengths greater than 1cm and appear somewhat like uneven dog's teeth. The dogtooth spar in the adjacent photo is approximately 30cm high.

REFERENCES

Atkinson, A. and Atkinson V. 1995. *Undara Volcano and its Lava Tubes.* Vernon and Anne Atkinson, Brisbane.

Branigan, D.F. and Packham, G.H. 2000. Field Geology of New South Wales. Department of Mineral Resources New South Wales, Sydney.

Cartoscope Pty Ltd. *Geological Sites of NSW.* www.geomaps.com.au

Ferrett, R.R. 2016. *Australia's Volcanoes.* New Holland Publishers, Sydney.

Field Geology Club of South Australia. 1997. *A Field Guide to the Geology of Yorke Peninsula.* Field Geology Club of South Australia Inc. Adelaide.

Finlayson, D.M. *et al.* 2008. *A Geological Guide to Canberra Region and Namadji National Park.* Geological Society of Australia, Canberra.

Henderson, R. and Johnson, D. 2016. *The Geology of Australia.* Cambridge University Press, Port Melbourne, Victoria.

Hoatson, D. M. *et al.* 1997. *Bungle Bungle Range.* Australian Geological Survey Organisation, Canberra.

Hoatson, D. M. *et al.* 2000. *Kakadu and Nitmiluk.* Australian Geological Survey Organisation, Canberra.

Lane, P. 2013. *Geology of Western Australia's National Parks.* Peter Lane, Margaret River, WA.

Lech, M.E. and Trewin, C.L. 2016. *Weathering, erosion, landforms and regolith.* Geoscience Australia, Canberra.

Manchester, P.S. 2010. *Created from Chaos.* Peter S Manchester, Norwood, Tasmania.

Struckmeyer, H. and Totterdell, J. *et al.* 1992. *Australia Evolution of a Continent.* Bureau of Mineral Resources, Canberra.

Willmott, W.F. 2014. *Rocks and Landscapes of the National Parks of Southern Queensland.* Geological Society of Australia, Queensland Division, Brisbane.

Willmott, W.F. 2006. *Rocks and Landscapes of the National Parks of Central Queensland.* Geological Society of Australia, Queensland Division, Brisbane.

Willmott, W.F. 2009. *Rocks and Landscapes of the National Parks of North Queensland.* Geological Society of Australia, Queensland Division, Brisbane.

First published in 2022 by Reed New Holland Publishers
Sydney

Level 1, 178 Fox Valley Road, Wahroonga, NSW 2076, Australia

newhollandpublishers.com

A record of this book is held at the National Library of Australia.

ISBN 978 1 92554 687 3

Managing Director: Fiona Schultz
Publisher and Project Editor: Simon Papps
Designer: Andrew Davies
Production Director: Arlene Gippert
Printed in China

10 9 8 7 6 5 4 3 2 1

Also available from Reed New Holland:

Australia's Volcanoes
Russell Ferrett
ISBN 978 1 92151 791 4

Gemstones and Minerals of Australia
Lin and Gayle Sutherland
ISBN 978 1 92151 729 7

For details of hundreds of other Natural History titles see newhollandpublishers.com

Keep up with Reed New Holland and New Holland Publishers on Facebook and Instagram

 facebook.com/ReedNewHolland and facebook.com/NewHollandPublishers

 NewHollandPublishers